TEXAS
LAW OF CONTRACTS

Second Edition

ASHLEY
CROWN
SYSTEMS, INC.

This publication is designed to provide accurate and current information regarding the subject matter covered. The principles and conclusions presented are subject to local, state and federal laws and regulations, court cases and revisions of same. If legal advice or other expert assistance is required, the reader is urged to consult a competent professional in the field.

Real Estate Publisher
Leigh Conway

Academic Information Analyst
Laura King

Technical Writer
Ben Hernandez

Technical Writer/Copyeditor
Sue Carlson

Graphic Designer
Susan Mackessy

©2010 by Ashley Crown Systems, Inc. a division of Allied Business Schools, Inc.
Second Edition
ISBN: 978-0934772-26-6

Ashley Crown Systems, Inc.
22952 Alcalde Drive
Laguna Hills, California 92653

Printed in the United States of America

CONTENTS

Preface .... *viii*
Acknowledgements .... *viii*

Unit 1: The Real Estate License Act 1
Introduction 1
Importance of Contracts 1
    Protect Your Client 2
    Protect Yourself 2
The Real Estate License Act 2
    Professional Ethics 2
    Unauthorized Practice of Law 4
    Texas Real Estate Broker-Lawyer Committee 5
Promulgated Contract Forms 6
    TREC Promulgated Forms 6
    Completion Instructions 7
    Exceptions to Using Promulgated Forms 9
Summary 10

Unit 2: Contract Basics 11
Introduction 11
Defining a Contract 11
Types of Contracts 11
    Express Contract 12
    Implied Contract 12
    Bilateral Contract 12
    Unilateral Contract.. 12
    Executory Contract 12
    Executed Contract 12
Contract Status 13
Valid Contract Requirements 13
    1. Legal Competency of Parties 14
    2. Mutual Consent 14
    3. Lawful Objective 16
    4. Consideration 16
    5. In Writing with Signatures of Parties 17
    6. Legal Description 17
Discharge of Contracts 17
    Performance 18
    Release 19
    Mutual Rescission 19

      Assignment 19
      Novation 19
      Breach 19
   Listing Agreements, Purchase Agreements, and Counteroffers 20
      Listing Agreements 20
      Purchase Agreements... 21
      Counteroffers 21
   Summary 22

Unit 3: Agency Relationships **25**
   Introduction 25
   What is Agency? 25
      Agency Relationships in Real Estate 26
      Disclosing Agency Relationship 30
      Creating Agency Relationship 31
      Terminating Agency Relationship 35
   Summary 36

Unit 4: Listing Agreements **37**
   Introduction 37
   Types of Listing Agreements 37
      Open Listing 37
      Net Listing 38
      Exclusive Agency Listing 38
      Exclusive Right to Sell Listing 38
   Summary 56

Unit 5: Buyer Representation Agreement **59**
   Introduction 59
   Buyer Representation 59
      Residential Buyer/Tenant Representation Agreement 60
   Summary 71

Unit 6: Residential Purchase Agreement **73**
   Introduction 73
   Sales Contracts in Real Estate 73
      The Offer and Acceptance 74
      Earnest Money 74
      Equitable Title 74
   One To Four Family Residential Contract (Resale) 74
   Case Study 84
      The Sellers 84
      Seller's Broker 84
      The Buyers 85
      Buyers' Broker 85
      Other Stipulations 85
      Completing the Form 86

Other Sales Contracts 98
    Residential Condominium Contract (Resale) 99
    New Home Contract (Incomplete Construction) 99
    New Home Contract (Completed Construction) 99
    Unimproved Property Contract 100
    Farm and Ranch Contract 100
Summary 100

Unit 7: Purchase Agreement Addenda **103**
Introduction 103
Addenda in Real Estate Contracts 103
    Basic Requirements 103
    Contingencies 104
    Disclosures 104
Promulgated Addendum Forms 105
    Addendum for Sale of Other Property by Buyer 105
    Addendum for "Back-Up" Contract 106
    Release of Liability on Assumed Loan and/or Restoration
    of Seller's VA Entitlement 106
    Seller's Temporary Residential Lease 107
    Buyer's Temporary Residential Lease 107
    Seller Financing Addendum 108
    Addendum for Coastal Area Property 109
    Addendum for Property Located Seaward of the Gulf
    Intracoastal Waterway 109
    Addendum for Property Subject to Mandatory Membership
    in an Owners' Association 109
    Subdivision Information, Including Resale Certificate for
    Property Subject to Mandatory Membership in an Owners'
    Association 110
    Notice of Termination of Contract 110
    Amendment 110
    Third Party Financing Condition Addendum 111
    Loan Assumption Addendum 112
    Notice to Prospective Buyer 113
Summary 113

Unit 8: Lease Agreements **115**
Introduction 115
Defining a Lease 115
Requirements of a Valid Lease 115
Types of Leasehold Estates 116
    Estate for Years 116
    Periodic Estates 116
    Tenancy at Will 117
    Tenancy at Sufferance 117
Residential Lease Agreement Form 117

1. Parties 132
2. Property 132
3. Term 132
4. Automatic Renewal and Notice of Termination 132
5. Rent 133
6. Late Charges 133
7. Returned Checks 133
8. Application of Funds 133
9. Pets 134
10. Security Deposit 134
11. Utilities 134
12. Use and Occupancy 135
13. Parking Rules 135
14. Access by Landlord 135
15. Move-In Condition 136
16. Move-Out 136
17. Property Maintenance 136
18. Repairs 136
19. Security Devices and Exterior Door Locks 137
20. Smoke Detectors 137
21. Liability 137
22. Holdover 138
23. Residential Landlord's Lien 138
24. Subordination 138
25. Casualty Loss or Condemnation 138
26. Special Provisions 138
27. Default 138
28. Early Termination 139
29. Attorney's Fees 139
30. Representations 139
31. Addenda 139
32. Notices 139
33. Agreement of Parties.. 140
34. Information 140
Summary 141

Unit 9: Real Estate Disclosures **143**
Introduction 143
Disclosures Required in Agency Relationships 143
   Information about Brokerage Services 144
Disclosures Required in Real Estate Transfers 145
   Seller's Disclosure of Property Condition 145
   Additional Statutory Disclosures 149
   Furnishing Controlling Documents 150
   Stigmatized Property 150
   Interstate Land Sales Full Disclosure Act 151
Disclosures in Financing 151

Truth in Lending Act (Reg Z) Disclosures 151
Real Estate Settlement Procedures Act Disclosures 152
Equal Credit Opportunity Act 152
Other Disclosures 152
Pest Control Inspection and Certification Reports 152
Foreign Investment in Real Property Tax Act (FIRPTA) 153
Home Inspection Notice 154
Notice Regarding the Advisability of Title Insurance 154
Commissions 154
Summary 154

Unit 10: Closing and Escrow Contracts **157**
Introduction 157
Closing Documents and Costs 157
Closing Documents 158
Real Estate Financing 159
Closing Costs 161
Escrow 161
The Escrow Agent 162
Basic Requirements for a Valid Escrow 162
General Escrow Principles and Rules 163
Escrow Procedures 163
Summary 167

PREFACE

Knowledge of contracts and contract law is mandatory in the real estate industry. While the text will benefit the real estate student, consumers and investors will also find the material useful.

The text is divided into units and the content is reinforced with samples of actual real estate contracts. Important terms are highlighted in **bold type** within each unit. Furthermore, each unit ends in a summary.

ACKNOWLEDGEMENTS

Texas Law of Contracts was the result of teamwork from the publisher, educators, and other professionals to make this introductory course the best in Texas real estate.

Ashley Crown would like to thank the following Texas real estate educators and consultants for their knowledge, expertise, and experience in real estate education: Bill Proctor, Broker-REALTOR®, and Professor at North Lake College in Irving, Texas; and Mary Ann Wheeler, Broker-REALTOR®.

Unit 1

The Real Estate License Act

Introduction

Real estate licensees must adhere to specific laws and regulatory codes when working with contracts. In 1939, the state of Texas passed The Real Estate License Act (TRELA) to regulate real estate practice. The primary reason for the Act was to protect the consumer from unscrupulous licensees. TRELA established procedures for licensing and laid the legal groundwork for the regulation of real estate practice. This unit explains the primary requirements of TRELA and how they relate to the regulation of real estate contracts.

Learning Objectives

After reading this unit, you should be able to:

- explain the importance of real estate contracts.
- discuss TRELA.
- discuss professional ethics requirements under TRELA.
- identify mandatory forms required by the Texas Real Estate Commission (TREC).

Importance of Contracts

A contract is a legally enforceable agreement created by separate parties to perform or not perform a certain act. In a real estate transaction, a contract is used to transfer or indicate an interest in real property.

A real estate contract is important because it clearly identifies the parties and the property, sets forth the rights and obligations of the parties, and provides a written record of the transaction.

Unfortunately, many buyers and sellers enter into real estate contracts without paying careful attention to the "small print". Most rely on a real estate licensee to fill out the documents. Therefore, it is critical that you understand common Texas contracts and related laws. A well-written contract will go a long way toward protecting the interests of all concerned parties.

Protect Your Client

When you fill out a contract correctly, you protect your client's interests. You help ensure that your client receives what he or she expects from the transaction and you help avoid common mistakes. For example, a strong contract can increase the likelihood that your client receives property that is structurally sound, has plumbing in good working condition, and is free of termites.

Protect Yourself

By paying careful attention to contract details, you can limit your own liability and receive what you expect from a real estate transaction.

> Example: Finally, after weeks of constant contact, you convince the seller of a prime piece of real estate to sign a listing agreement with you. Overcome with joy, you haphazardly fill out the agreement with the seller. Two months later, after much hard work, you find a solid buyer. Then you begin thinking about all the fabulous things you will do with the large commission you will receive. However, on closing day you learn from the escrow agent that the closing went well but you will not be paid. Apparently, while filling out the listing agreement, you skipped a section that specified your fee for selling the property.

This type of situation can be avoided when dealing with real estate contracts if you use what you will learn in this course, exercise caution, and implement due diligence.

The Real Estate License Act

The Real Estate License Act (TRELA), enacted in 1939, was developed not only to regulate licensing but also to provide ground rules for licensees filling out and reviewing contracts.

TRELA regulates those who sell, exchange, procure, prospect, or inspect real property for a fee or other valuable consideration. Brokers must closely monitor the professional and vocational acts of their licensed staff because TRELA holds brokers responsible for all acts performed by any real estate salesperson associated with or acting for the broker.

Professional Ethics

The Texas Real Estate Commission (TREC) advocates several canons of professional ethics and conduct for real estate licensees. The primary characteristics licensees must exhibit are fidelity, integrity, and competency.

Fidelity

The broker or salesperson is placed in a position of trust; therefore, he or she is obligated to exhibit fidelity, or faithfulness, to the principal when considering his or her interests. A real estate licensee, while acting as an agent for another, is a fiduciary. Special obligations are imposed when such a fiduciary relationship is created.

Fiduciary Responsibilities

- The primary duty of the real estate agent is to represent the interests of the client; his or her position as an agent should be revealed to all parties concerned in a real estate transaction. While in the midst of performing duties, the agent should treat other parties to a transaction fairly.

- The real estate agent must be faithful and observant to the trust placed in him or her and be scrupulous and meticulous in performing his or her functions.

- The real estate agent must not place any personal interest above that of his or her client.

Integrity

A real estate broker or salesperson has a special obligation to exercise integrity in the discharge of his or her responsibilities. Integrity includes the use of prudence and caution when dealing on the principal's behalf. Practicing integrity helps avoid misrepresentation, in any way, by acts of commission or omission.

Competency

A real estate broker or salesperson must be competent. Competency is the obligation of a real estate licensee to be knowledgeable as a real estate practitioner.

Characteristics of Competent Real Estate Brokers and Salespeople

- Keep informed about national, state, and local issues and developments in the real estate industry.

- Exercise good judgment and skill in the performance of his or her work.

- Work with a variety of clients and customers.

- Follow anti-discrimination concepts, rules, and regulations.

- Take continuing education courses about new legislation and trends in real estate.

Unauthorized Practice of Law

TREC's rules and the TRELA were created to protect the public. TRELA Section 16 of The Real Estate License Act prohibits a licensee from providing legal counsel to his or her client, as does Article 13 of the National Association of REALTORS® Code of Ethics. The National Association of REALTORS® (NAR) is a real estate trade association. A member of NAR is known as a REALTOR® and must follow NAR's rules and Code of Ethics. These rules are important when discussing contracts because, while a licensee cannot practice law, he or she can legally complete contract forms involving real estate.

TRELA Section 16

TRELA Section 16 does not allow a licensee to provide legal counsel or create his or her own forms. It permits a licensee to complete a contract form that may bind the sale, exchange, option, lease, or rental of any interest in real property. The forms used in these transactions must have been prepared by the property owner, prepared by an attorney, or promulgated by the Texas Real Estate Commission. This unit will discuss these exceptions in detail later.

Section 16 (a) of TRELA states what will happen to you if you do not follow these rules.

(a) A license granted under the provisions of this Act shall be suspended or revoked by the commission on proof that the licensee, not being licensed and authorized to practice law in this state, for a consideration, reward, pecuniary benefit, present or anticipated, direct or indirect, or in connection with or as part of his employment, agency, or fiduciary relationship as a licensee, drew a deed, note, deed of trust, will, or other written instrument that may transfer or anywise affect the title to or an interest in land, except as provided in the subsections below, or advised or counseled a person as to the validity or legal sufficiency of an instrument or as to the validity of title to real estate.

Section 16 (b) tells you how to properly complete contract forms.

(b) . . . the completion of contract forms which bind the sale, exchange, option, lease, or rental of any interest in real property by a real estate broker or salesperson incident to the performance of the acts of a broker . . . does not constitute the unauthorized or illegal practice of law in this state, provided the forms have been promulgated for use by the commission for the particular kind of transaction involved, or the forms have been prepared by an attorney at law licensed by this state and approved by said attorney for the particular kind of transaction involved, or the forms have been prepared by the property owner or prepared by an attorney and required by the property owner.

NAR Code of Ethics

REALTORS® are also subject to the NAR Code of Ethics, which are rules of professional conduct. Article 13 of the Code of Ethics addresses the unauthorized practice of law as follows:

REALTORS® may not engage in activities that constitute the unauthorized practice of law and must recommend that legal counsel be obtained when the interest of any party to the transaction requires it.

If you find yourself in a situation that may put you in violation of TRELA Section 16 and/or Article 13 of the NAR Code of Ethics, tell the principal to seek the advice of an attorney. Even if you are knowledgeable in a specific legal topic, be careful never to offer legal advice to a principal.

In addition to prohibiting legal advice, Section 16 (a) of TRELA also adds that it is illegal for a licensee to create a deed, note, deed of trust, will, or other written instrument that transfers or may transfer an interest or title to real property.

Texas Real Estate Broker-Lawyer Committee

The Texas legislature created the Texas Real Estate Broker-Lawyer Committee (Committee), an advisory body that develops and recommends various contract forms to TREC for use by licensees. TRELA Section 16 (c) and (d) describe the Committee in the following ways:

(c) A Texas Real Estate Broker-Lawyer Committee is hereby created which, in addition to other powers and duties delegated to it, shall draft and revise contract forms capable of standardization for use by real estate licensees and which will expedite real estate transactions and reduce controversies to a minimum while containing safeguards adequate to protect the interest of the principals to the transaction.

(d) The Texas Real Estate Broker-Lawyer Committee shall have 12 members including six members appointed by the commission and six members of the State Bar of Texas appointed by the President of the State Bar of Texas.

The forms created by the Committee are not mandatory, since TREC ultimately has rule-making authority. The Committee merely develops and recommends their adoption. The Real Estate License Act established the responsibilities of the committee, which is composed of six brokers who are appointed by TREC and six attorneys appointed by the president of the State Bar of Texas. The Texas legislature also gave the commission rule-making authority and that the rules of the commission are just as binding for licensees as are the provisions of the act.

Promulgated Contract Forms

To help licensees avoid the unauthorized practice of law, the commission has promulgated these forms to be used for all transactions assisted by licensees, unless the transaction meets one of the exceptions defined by TREC rules.

The Texas Real Estate Commission (TREC) may adopt legislation that requires real estate licensees to use promulgated (mandatory) contract forms prepared by the Texas Real Estate Broker-Lawyer Committee. A licensee must use a promulgated form when negotiating contracts that bind the sale, exchange, option, lease, or rental of any interest in real property.

TREC Rule 537.11 lists the forms currently promulgated for mandatory use by licensees and gives the instructions for completing the forms. TREC has the power to suspend or revoke a real estate license if it is determined that a licensee failed to use a promulgated contract form for a specific contract situation.

TREC Promulgated Forms

The different promulgated forms for real estate use are listed in TREC Rule 537.11. It includes name and reference number of the form along with the date the form was adopted and the date of any amendments. Do not use earlier versions of a form. Doing so is an unlawful, unauthorized practice of law. The current forms may be found at the TREC website: http://www.trec.state.tx.us/ and then select the tab labeled "Forms, Laws & Contracts".

Promulgated Contracts

Number	Name
9-7	Unimproved Property Contract
20-8	One to Four Family Residential Contract (Resale)
23-9	New Home Contract (Incomplete Construction)
24-9	New Home Contract (Completed Construction)
25-6	Farm and Ranch Contract
30-7	Residential Condominium Contract (Resale)

Promulgated Addenda

Number	Name
10-5	Addendum for Sale of Other Property by Buyer
11-6	Addendum for "Back-Up" Contract
12-2	Addendum for Release of Liability on Assumed Loan and/or Restoration of Seller's VA Entitlement
15-4	Seller's Temporary Residential Lease

16-4	Buyer's Temporary Residential Lease
26-5	Seller Financing Addendum
28-1	Environmental Assessment, Threatened or Endangered Species, and Wetlands Addendum
33-1	Addendum for Coastal Area Property
34-3	Addendum for Property Located Seaward of the Gulf Intracoastal Waterway
36-5	Addendum for Property Subject to Mandatory Membership in an Owners' Association
39-6	Amendment to Contract
40-3	Third Party Financing Condition Addendum
41-1	Loan Assumption Addendum
44-0	Addendum for Reservation of Oil, Gas and Other Minerals
45-0	Short Sale Addendum

Promulgated Resale Certificates
Number Name

| 32-2 | Condominium Resale Certificate |
| 37-3 | Subdivision Information, Including Resale Certificate for Property Subject to Membership in a Property Owners' Association |

Promulgated Notice
Number Name

| 38-2 | Notice of Termination of Contract |

Optional/Voluntary Use Forms
Number Name

OP-C	Notice to Prospective Buyer
OP-H	Seller's Disclosure of Property Condition
OP-I	Texas Real Estate Consumer Notice Concerning Hazards or Repairs
OP-K	Information About Brokerage Services
OP-L	Lead-Based Paint Addendum

Completion Instructions

A licensee should become familiar with what the rules permit and prohibit before completing any contract forms that bind a sale, lease, temporary lease, or rental of real property. TRELA has several rules that licensees should follow when completing promulgated contracts.

How You Should Fill Out Promulgated Contracts

1. Do not draw or prepare contracts fixing and defining the legal rights of the principals to a transaction.

2. When negotiating certain real estate transactions, you may complete forms approved and promulgated by TREC or forms otherwise permitted by these rules.

3. When filling out a promulgated form, you may only fill in the blanks provided and may not add to or delete items from the form. However, you may add factual statements and business details desired by principals. In addition, you may delete items requested by a principal in order to make the contract conform to his or her intentions.

4. Do not add to a promulgated earnest money contract form any factual statements or business details that are already contained in an addendum, lease, or other form promulgated by TREC.

5. Do not offer or give legal advice. However, you may explain to a principal the meaning of the factual statements and business details contained in a contract.

6. Use contract forms prepared by the Texas Real Estate Broker-Lawyer Committee and approved by TREC that replace outdated forms.

7. Consult an attorney prior to the execution of a contract if there are unusual matters in the contract that can only be resolved through legal counsel.

8. Advise the parties to a contract that it is a binding document.

9. Reproduce forms approved or promulgated by TREC from any of the following sources and adhere to the following formats:

    *   numbered copies obtained from the commission, whether in a printed format or electronically reproduced from the files available on the commission's Internet site.

    *   printed copies made from copies obtained from the commission.

    *   legible photocopies made from such copies.

    *   electronically printed through a computer.

10. Adhere to the following formats for copies printed from a computer:

    *   the computer file or program containing the form text must not allow the end-user direct access to the text of the form and may only permit the user to insert language in the blanks in the forms or to strike through language at the direction of the parties to the contract.

    *   typefaces or fonts must appear to be identical to those used by the commission in printed copies of the particular form.

    *   the text and number of pages must be identical to that used by the commission in printed proofs of the particular form.

- the spacing, length of blanks, borders, and placement of text on the page must appear to be identical to that used by the commission in printed copies of the form.
- the name and address of the person or firm responsible for developing the software program must be legibly printed below the border at the bottom of each page in no less than 6-point type and in no larger than 10-point type.
- the text of the form must be obtained from a copy of the form bearing a control number assigned by the commission.
- the control number of each copy must appear on all forms reproduced from the copy, including forms reproduced by computer-driven printers.

11. Reproduce forms approved or promulgated by the commission be on the same sized paper used by the commission, with the following changes or additions only.

- The business name or logo of a broker, organization, or printer may appear at the top of a form outside the border.
- The broker's name may be inserted in any blank provided for that purpose.

Exceptions to Using Promulgated Forms

At times, you do not need to use a promulgated TREC form. Examples of these times include:

- transactions in which the licensee is functioning solely as a principal, not an agent.
- transactions in which an agency of the U.S. government requires a different form to be used.
- transactions for which a contract form has been prepared by the property owner or prepared by an attorney and required by the property owner.
- transactions for which no standard contract form has been promulgated by TREC, and the licensee uses a form prepared by an attorney licensed by Texas and approved by the attorney for the particular kind of transactions involved or prepared by the Texas Real Estate Broker-Lawyer Committee and made available for trial use by licensees with the consent of TREC.

Summary

The Real Estate License Act regulates real estate licensees, especially when they work with contracts. TREC promulgates several canons of professional ethics and conduct for real estate licensees. The main characteristics that licensees must exhibit are fidelity, integrity, and competency.

The Texas legislature created the Texas Real Estate Broker-Lawyer Committee to act as an advisory body to develop and recommend various contract forms to TREC to be used by licensees when performing the tasks for which they have been licensed. In the best interest of the public, the commission may adopt rules and regulations requiring real estate brokers and salespersons to use contract forms prepared by the Texas Real Estate Broker-Lawyer Committee and promulgated by the commission.

The first part of Rule 537.11 lists the forms that are currently promulgated for mandatory use by licensees for particular transactions. The second part of the rule offers instructions on how a real estate licensee should complete a promulgated form. Licensees should be aware of these different types of forms promulgated by TREC.

Unit 2
Contract Basics

Introduction

Real estate licensees encounter a variety of contracts. Whether a contract is used to purchase real estate or lease property, you must understand its purpose, know how to complete it, and be able to explain the content to clients. This unit explains what a contract is, exposes you to various types of contracts, explores components used to create valid contracts, and explains how contracts are performed and discharged.

Learning Objectives

After reading this unit, you should be able to:

- define a real estate contract and common contract terms.
- identify different types of contracts.
- name the requirements of a valid contract.
- explain how a contract is discharged.
- identify common real estate contracts.

Defining a Contract

A **contract** is an agreement created by separate parties to perform or not perform certain acts. Each party promises to perform the acts under the terms of the contract. In a real estate transaction, a contract is used to transfer or indicate an interest in real property. For example, in a **listing agreement**, the seller of a property promises to pay a commission to a broker who finds a buyer.

Types of Contracts

A contract may be express, implied, bilateral, or unilateral; it may also be executory or executed.

Express Contract

In an **express contract**, the parties declare the terms of the agreement and put their intentions in words, either orally or in writing. An example of an express contract is a lease or rental agreement in which the landlord agrees to allow the tenant to live on the property and the tenant agrees to pay rent in return.

Implied Contract

When a contract is implied, the agreement is demonstrated by conduct rather than by words. For example, when you go into a restaurant and order food, you create an **implied contract**. By requesting a service, it is implied that you will pay for the service.

Bilateral Contract

A **bilateral contract** is an agreement in which each party promises to perform an act in exchange for the other party's promise to perform their part of the agreement. In other words, for the contract to be completed, each party must keep the agreement. For example, in a real estate transaction, the buyer promises to pay a certain amount of money and the seller agrees to transfer title to the property in exchange for that money. The contract is not complete until the seller has his or her money and the buyer holds title to the property.

Unilateral Contract

A contract in which a party promises to perform without the expectation that the other party will perform is called a **unilateral contract**. The second party is not obligated to act, but if he or she does, the first party must keep their promise. For example, a neighbor who is missing a pet may post signs offering a reward for the return of the pet. If the pet is returned, the neighbor is required to pay the promised reward.

Executory Contract

A contract that remains to be performed by one or both parties is referred to as an **executory contract**. An example of an executory contract is an escrow that is not yet closed or a contract that has not been signed by both parties.

Executed Contract

A contract is executed when all parties have performed according to the agreement. Performance may be as simple as signing the document. An **executed contract** is a sales agreement that has been signed by all parties involved in the transaction.

Contract Status

The status of a contract can be valid, unenforceable, void, or voidable. A **valid** or **enforceable** contract is binding on the parties and has all basic elements required by law for a contract. An **unenforceable contract** is an agreement that will not stand up to legal challenge due to the incapacity of a party, illegal contract terms, or the presence of undue influence upon a party, which caused that party to sign the contract. According to the Statute of Frauds, an example of an unenforceable contract is an oral agreement that must be in writing.

A contract is **void** if there is no contract at all, or no legal effect. This may occur due to lack of capacity of one or both parties, or if the subject of the contract is illegal. A **voidable** contract is valid and enforceable, but may be rejected by one or both parties if it was induced by fraud, menace, or duress.

Who May Void a Contract?

- If the contract was entered into with a minor, the minor may void it.
- If it can be proven that fraud has been committed, the nonfraudulent party may void the contract.
- The buyer may void the contract if the seller fails to provide the buyer with a copy of the "Seller's Disclosure of Property Condition" as required by Section 5.008 of the Texas Property Code. If the disclosure is provided after the agreement is signed, the buyer may terminate the contract within seven days after receipt of the disclosure.
- The buyer has an unrestricted right to terminate the contract per Section 5.012 of the Texas Property Code if the buyer is not provided with homeowner's association information and a "Resale Certificate" prior to creating a purchase contract.
- If a seller does not provide the buyer with appropriate notice prior to creating a purchase contract involving property that is situated in a utility district or other district that provides water, sewage, drainage, or flood control, the buyer may void the contract under Chapter 49 of the Texas Water Code.

Valid Contract Requirements

In Texas, a contract must meet six requirements to be valid. The contract must have legally competent parties, mutual consent between the parties, a lawful objective, sufficient consideration, it must be in writing and be signed by the parties, and it must contain a legal description.

1. Legal Competency of Parties

Parties entering into a contract must be legally capable or competent. To be legally competent, a person must be at least 18 years old, unless they are married, in the military, or have been declared emancipated by the court.

A minor is not legally capable of creating an agency agreement with a broker to buy or sell property, and any contract made with a minor is considered voidable by the minor. A broker dealing with a minor should consult an attorney and proceed cautiously.

If a person who is declared legally incompetent enters into a contract, that contract will be terminated. If it is obvious that a person does not comprehend the situation, terms of the agreement, or the significance of the contract, there can be no contract. If the person is declared incompetent, a court-appointed guardian would have legal capacity to enter into contracts on behalf of the individual. Minors and incompetents may acquire title to real property by gift or inheritance; however, any transfer of property must be approved by the courts prior to the execution of the contract.

If a person makes a contract while intoxicated or under the influence of legal or illegal drugs, the contract can be voided when the individual regains sobriety. However, the contract may also be ratified, or approved after the fact, depending on the parties.

Any person may give another the authority to act on his or her behalf. The legal document that creates this relationship is called a **power of attorney**. The person holding the power of attorney is an **attorney-in-fact**. A power of attorney is useful, for example, when a buyer or seller is out of town and trusts the attorney-in-fact to operate on his or her behalf. When dealing with real property, a power of attorney must be recorded to be valid, and is good for as long as the **principal** is competent. A power of attorney may be cancelled by the principal at any time by recording a revocation.

2. Mutual Consent

In a valid contract, all parties must mutually agree or have **mutual consent**. Mutual consent (or mutual assent) is sometimes known as a **meeting of the minds**. It is an offer by one party and acceptance by the other party or simply an **offer and acceptance**. Mutual consent must include **genuine assent**, which means that the offer and acceptance was genuine and freely made by all parties.

Offer and Acceptance

An **offer** shows the contractual intent of the **offeror**, or the person making the offer, to enter into a contract. That offer must be communicated to the offeree, or the person to whom the offer is being made. Unconditional acceptance of the offer is necessary for all parties to be legally bound. The offer must be definite and certain in its terms, and the agreement must be genuine, or the contract may be voidable by one or both parties. One party must offer and another must accept, without condition.

An **acceptance** is an unqualified agreement to the terms of an offer. The offeree must agree to every item of the offer for the acceptance to be complete. Acceptance of an offer must be communicated to the offeror, in the manner specified, before a contract becomes binding between the parties. The seller may rescind an offer prior to acceptance. Silence is not considered acceptance.

An offeror is hopeful that his or her offer is accepted in a **timely manner** and a contract created. An offer is specific, and an offeror does not have to wait indefinitely for an answer.

If the original terms in the acceptance change in any way, the offer becomes a **counteroffer**, and the first offer terminates. The person making the original offer is no longer bound by that offer, and may or may not accept the counteroffer. The counteroffer becomes a new offer made by the original offeree.

Genuine Assent

Another requirement for mutual consent is that the offer and acceptance are genuine and freely made by all parties. Genuine assent does not exist if there is fraud, misrepresentation, mistake, duress, menace, or undue influence involved in reaching an agreement.

Fraud

An act meant to deceive in order to get someone to part with something of value is called fraud. An outright lie or making a promise with no intention of carrying it out can be fraud. Lack of disclosure—causing someone to make or accept an offer—is also fraud. For example, it is fraud to fail to tell a prospective buyer who is making an offer that a property has known soil problems. Fraud can make the contract voidable.

Innocent Misrepresentation

When the person unknowingly provides wrong information, **innocent misrepresentation** occurs. Even though no dishonesty is involved, a contract may be rescinded or revoked by the party who feels misled. The **hold harmless clause** protects the broker from incorrect information.

Mistake

In contract law, a **mistake** is an incorrect understanding by one or more parties to a contract and may be used as grounds to invalidate the agreement. A mistake does not include ignorance, incompetence, or poor judgment. For example, a seller rushes through the reading of a sales contract and accepts an offer to purchase a home based on what he or she thinks is an all cash offer. Later, the seller discovers that he or she agreed to carry a second trust deed and there was no all cash offer. Even though the seller made a mistake in reading the sales contract, the seller is bound to the agreement due to his or her incompetence.

Duress

A contract entered into under duress is voidable. **Duress** exists where unlawful constraint or action is exercised on a person to force them to perform an act against their will.

Undue Influence

Using undue influence or unfair advantage is also unacceptable. **Undue influence** consists of using pressure to force someone to sign a contract. **Unfair advantage** exists when someone takes advantage of a relationship to get someone to sign a contract. Each will result in a contract that is voidable by the injured party.

3. Lawful Objective

Even if the parties are capable and mutually agreeable, the object of the contract must be lawful. A contract requiring the performance of an illegal act would not be valid, nor would a contract where the consideration was stolen.

The contract must also be legal in its formation and operation. For example, a note bearing an **interest rate** in excess of that allowed by law would be void. Contracts opposing good morals and general public policy are also unenforceable.

4. Consideration

Legally, every contract must have acceptable consideration. **Consideration** is something of value given by one party to a contract to another party in exchange for something of value. For example, a promise for a promise, money for a promise, money for property, or goods for services. Terms that denote **acceptable consideration** include valuable, adequate, good, or sufficient consideration.

Forbearance, or forgiving a debt or obligation, or giving up an interest or a right, qualifies as valuable consideration. Gifts, such as real property based solely on love and affection are good consideration. These gifts meet the legal requirement stating that consideration be present in a contract.

In an option, the promise of the offeror is the consideration for the forbearance desired from the offeree. In other words, the person wanting the option promises to give something of value in return for being able to exercise the option to purchase at some specifically named time in the future.

In a bilateral contract, a promise of one party is consideration for the promise of another. For example, in the sale of real property, the buyer promises to pay a certain amount and the seller promises to transfer title.

Note: The earnest money given at the time of an offer is not the consideration for the sale. It is simply an indication of the buyer's intent to perform the contract, and may be used for damages, even if the buyer backs out of the sale.

5. In Writing with Signatures of Parties

A valid contract must be in writing and signed by the parties. According to the **Statute of Frauds**, all agreements affecting title to or interest in real estate in Texas must meet this requirement to be enforceable. In Texas, an oral agreement for the sale of property is unenforceable and licensees are discouraged from conducting real estate negotiations in this way. All offers and counteroffers should be in writing. A binding executory contract does not exist until it has been made in writing, accepted, and the offeror has been informed of the acceptance. A lease for one year or less is the only exception because it does not have to be in writing.

6. Legal Description

Every valid contract must contain a **legal description**. A street address alone is not sufficient when supplying a legal description for a property. According to the Statute of Frauds, the legal description should be accurate and descriptive enough so that one could easily identify the property given the legal description alone. The recorded plat method (lot, block, section, and subdivision) and the metes and bounds method are the two most common forms of legal description.

Discharge of Contracts

Discharge of contract refers to the completion, cancellation, or termination of a contract. Contracts are discharged by performance, release, rescission, assignment, novation, and breach.

Performance

Commonly, the discharge of a contract occurs when the contract has been fully performed.

Tender of Performance

A **tender of performance** is an offer by one of the parties to carry out his or her part of the contract. Usually, a tender is made at a point in time close to escrow. The person to whom the tender is made must state any objections at that time or the objections will be **waived**. A **waiver** is the relinquishment or refusal to accept a right. A person must take advantage of his or her rights at the proper time. If they do not, they give up, or waive, their rights. A tender of performance by the buyer, for example, by depositing the purchase money into escrow, places the seller in default if the seller refuses to accept it and deliver a deed. The buyer could rescind the transaction or sue for breach of contract or for **specific performance**.

Time is of the Essence

Sometimes contracts specify that "time is of the essence" when performing the terms of the contract. When a contract calls for "time is of the essence", performance of the contract must be made within a reasonable amount of time. For example, if a contract involves the payment of money, the payment should be made immediately unless otherwise agreed by both parties.

Promulgated forms from the TREC require performance of the contract within a specified timeframe. The forms include actual dates and times in which specified parties must carry out the contract's provisions. This section is placed in the contract to emphasize that the time limits found in the contract must be met or the contract may be considered void.

The contract begins on the effective date, which is usually listed in the contract above the signatures. Failure to disclose the effective date results in the inability to determine whether performance on a contract was established. When both parties exercise good faith in performing the requirements of the contract within a reasonable timeframe, Texas courts will uphold the contract's provisions.

A TREC promulgated contract form has the "time is of the essence" clause in certain attached addenda—Addendum for Sale of Other Property by Buyer and the Addendum for Back-Up Contract.

Release

The person in the contract to whom an obligation is owed may release the other party from the obligation to perform the contract.

Mutual Rescission

A **mutual rescission** occurs when all parties to a contract agree to cancel the agreement.

Assignment

An assignment transfers all interests of the **assignor** (principal) to the **assignee**. The assignee is the individual who takes over the assignor's rights, remedies, benefits, and duties in the contract. In this situation, the assignor is not completely released from the contract obligations and remains secondarily liable.

Novation

If a party to a contract wants to be released entirely from any obligation for the contract, it may be done by novation. **Novation** is the substitution, by agreement, of a new obligation for an existing one, with the intent to extinguish the original contract. For example, novation occurs when a buyer assumes a seller's loan, and the lender releases the seller from the loan contract by substituting the buyer's name on the loan.

Breach

A **breach of contract** is a failure to perform on part or all of the terms and conditions of a contract without a legal excuse. A person harmed by non-performance can accept the failure to perform or has a choice of three remedies: unilateral rescission, lawsuit for money damages, or lawsuit for specific performance.

Unilateral Rescission

Unilateral rescission is available to a person who enters a contract without genuine assent because of fraud, mistake, duress, menace, undue influence, or faulty consideration. Rescission may be used as a means of discharging a contract by agreement.

If one party has been wronged by a breach of contract, the innocent party can stop performing all obligations as well, therefore unilaterally rescinding the contract. This must be done promptly, including restoring to the other party everything of value received because of the breached contract, on condition that the other party shall do the same.

Lawsuit for Money Damages

A second remedy for breach of contract is a **lawsuit for money damages**. If the damages to the injured party can be expressed in a dollar amount, the innocent party can sue for money damages, including the price paid by the buyer, the difference between the contract price and the value of the property, title and document expenses, consequential damages, and interest.

Lawsuit for Specific Performance

A third remedy for breach of contract is a **lawsuit for specific performance**. This is an action in court by the injured party to force the breaching party to carry out the remainder of the contract according to the agreed upon terms, price and conditions. Generally, this remedy occurs when money cannot restore an injured party's position. This is often the case in real estate because of the difficulty in finding a similar property.

Listing Agreements, Purchase Agreements, and Counteroffers

The most common types of contracts a licensee encounters are listing agreements, purchase agreements, and counteroffers. The real estate licensee should be familiar with the content of these contracts and be able to explain them to clients.

Listing Agreements

A **listing agreement** is a written contract by which a principal, or seller, employs a broker to sell real estate. When the seller signs a listing agreement promising payment for service by the listing broker and the broker promises to use due diligence in finding a buyer, it is a **bilateral contract** (a promise is given in exchange for a promise).

In the listing agreement, the seller promises to pay a commission upon presentation of a ready, willing, and able buyer who meets all the terms of the listing. A **ready, willing, and able** buyer is one who is prepared to enter into a purchase contract, eager to buy, and meets the financing requirements of purchase. A listing agreement gives the broker the right to be paid only after doing the job, or producing results. It is similar to an employment contract between the seller and the broker.

Under agency law, the listing broker is a **special agent** who deals in the name of the principal to negotiate the sale of property. The broker does not have control over the property itself, while acting within the course of a special agency, but only has the right to represent that principal. The seller does not promise to sell the house, nor can the seller be forced to sell, even after signing a listing agreement. The seller simply promises to pay a commission to the broker if he or she brings a ready, willing, and able buyer.

> Example: Ellen, a licensed real estate broker, spoke to everyone in her area at least once a month. Since she was well known, owner Sam called her when he wanted to sell his home. Ellen met with him and completed a listing agreement. An agency by express, written agreement was created.

Purchase Agreements

A **purchase agreement**, or sales contract, is the original agreement between the buyer and seller. Because of this, it reflects the mutual and agreed-upon desires of the parties when it becomes the actual escrow instructions.

Any mutual changes are made using an addendum to the original contract rather than amendments to escrow instructions. An escrow is opened when a real estate agent brings the signed purchase agreement to the escrow holder, who makes a copy and accepts it by signing off in the required box in the document. The escrow holder should be concerned about whether the contract is complete, fully signed, and initialed before accepting it. It must be a valid contract before becoming instructions for the escrow.

Once escrow instructions have been signed by the buyer and the seller and returned to the escrow holder, neither party may unilaterally change the escrow instructions. Any changes must be made by mutual agreement between the buyer and seller. The escrow agent does not have the authority to make changes in the contract upon the direction of either the buyer or the seller, unless both agree to the change in the form of an amendment or addendum to the purchase agreement.

The broker has no authority to amend or change any part of the escrow instructions without the knowledge of the principals. The written consent of both the buyer and the seller, in the form of an amendment to the original instructions or an amendment to the purchase agreement, must be given before any change can be made.

Counteroffers

When buyers make an offer to sellers, acceptance must be unconditional. An acceptance is an unqualified agreement to the terms of an offer. The one receiving the offer (offeree) must agree to every item of the offer for the acceptance to be complete.

If the seller does not agree to the terms of the offer, he or she can change the terms and resubmit them to the buyer for review. This process of rejecting the original purchase offer and submitting a new offer is known as a **counteroffer**. After a counteroffer, the person making the original offer is no longer bound by that offer, and may accept the counteroffer or not. The counteroffer becomes a new offer made by the original offeree.

Acceptance of a counteroffer must be communicated to the offeror, in the manner specified, before a contract becomes binding between the parties. A counteroffer may be rescinded prior to acceptance.

Termination of a Counteroffer
- Lapse of time - a counteroffer is revoked if the offeree fails to accept it within a prescribed period.
- Communication of notice of revocation: notice is filed by the counterofferor anytime before the other party has communicated acceptance.
- Failure of offeree to fulfill a condition of acceptance prescribed by the counterofferor.
- A qualified acceptance or counteroffer by the offeree.
- Rejection by the offeree.
- Death or insanity of the counterofferor or offeree.
- Unlawful object of the proposed contract.

Summary

In most real estate transactions, a **contract** is used to transfer or indicate an interest in real property. A real estate agent in Texas is expected to understand the various contract forms and explain them to clients.

A contract is an agreement created by separate parties to perform or not perform a certain act. Different types of contracts exist. A contract may be **express**, **implied**, **bilateral**, or **unilateral**. It may also be **executory** or **executed**; and **void**, **voidable**, **unenforceable**, or **valid**.

A contract must meet six requirements to be valid. The contract must have legally **competent parties**, **mutual consent** between the parties, a **lawful objective**, **sufficient consideration**, it must be **in writing** and be **signed by the parties**, and it must **contain a legal description**.

A contract is void if there is no contract at all or no legal effect. This may occur because of lack of capacity of one or both of the parties or the subject of the contract is illegal. **Discharge** of contract refers to the cancellation or termination of a contract. Discharging a contract can be accomplished by **performance**, **release**, **rescission**, **assignment**, **novation**, and **breach**.

The most common contracts a real estate licensee encounters are **listing agreements**, **purchase agreements**, and **counteroffers**. You should be familiar with the content of these contracts and be able to explain them to clients.

Unit 3
Agency Relationships

Introduction

As a licensee, your main job will be to represent someone else in a real estate transaction. When that person gives you authority to act on his or her behalf, a special legal relationship is created, called an agency, which is defined by a body of laws called agency law. This unit discusses the different types of relationships a licensee can form with a client and the contracts that set up the relationships. These relationships are called **agency relationships**.

Agency law will affect all of your agency relationships and help you determine whom you represent and what your obligations are when acting for that person. Your success in real estate sales will depend on your knowledge of agency law. Consumers will rely on you to explain the law as well as to make sure it is carried out. They will want to be assured that you are representing their best interests.

Learning Objectives

After reading this unit, you should be able to:

- explain the concept of an agency relationship.
- define agency and list two reasons for creating an agency.
- describe the fiduciary relationship between the principal and real estate broker.
- discuss termination of agency.

What is Agency?

Agency is a legal relationship in which a principal authorizes an agent to act as the principal's representative when dealing with third parties. A **principal** in a sales transaction is either the buyer or seller. The **agent** is one who has a fiduciary duty of loyalty, integrity, and utmost care to the principal.

A **fiduciary relationship** exists between the agent and the principal. A fiduciary relationship implies a position of trust or confidence. The agent is in a position of trust or confidence with the principal and owes the principal certain fiduciary duties.

The agent is bound by agency law to act in the best interests of the principal. There is an obligation always to act fairly and honestly with third parties. A **third party** is anyone the licensee is not legally obligated to provide with his or her advice, opinion, or loyalty.

The agent works for the principal and with third parties.

An agent is either a special agent or general agent. This depends on the scope of authority delegated to the agent by the principal. A **special agent** is employed to perform a specific task, whereas any other agent would be a **general agent**. A real estate broker, for example, who has a contract is a special agent authorized to perform certain acts for a specified time.

The authority given an agent is determined by the principal. If described in a written agreement, it is called **actual authority**. A principal is not responsible for the acts of the agent if those acts are beyond the agent's actual authority. If the principal has not given the agent actual or ostensible (apparent) authority to do the act, a third party cannot hold the principal responsible.

An agent may have authority under a power of attorney, allowing him or her to conduct certain business for a principal. A **power of attorney** is a written document that gives a person legal authority to act on behalf of another person. Typically, the two types used in real estate are special and general. A **special power of attorney** authorizes the agent to do certain specific acts. A **general power of attorney** allows the agent to transact all the business of the principal. The agent is then known as an attorney-in-fact.

Agency Relationships in Real Estate

Most agency relationships have a principal, an agent, and a third party. In a real estate transaction the **principal** (buyer or seller), **agent** (real estate broker), and **third party** (customer) are bound together in a legal relationship, with all the duties and rights that go with that connection.

Brokers have an agency relationship and fiduciary duties to the seller when they enter into a listing agreement. Buyers who complete a "Buyer's Representation" agreement enter into an agency relationship with the broker, obligating the broker to provide fiduciary duties to the buyer. A listing agreement and buyer's representation agreement are both employment contracts. Both are express contracts with confidentiality of all information learned to extend to perpetuity, regardless of the transference of any fees for services rendered.

Most frequently, the principal is a seller who employs an agent to find a buyer for his or her property. Sometimes the principal is a buyer who employs an agent to locate a property.

The Broker is the Agent

The principal's agent is always a licensed real estate broker, never a salesperson. That is why a listing broker is also called a **listing agent**; a selling broker is also called a **selling agent**; and a buyer's broker is also called a **buyer's agent**. When a broker represents only the buyer or the seller in the transaction, it is called **single agency**. A **dual agency** exists if one broker represents both principals in the transaction. However, since September 2005, The Real Estate License Act (TRELA) does not allow a broker to act as a dual agent. Instead, brokers need to act as intermediaries if they are representing both buyer and seller. An **intermediary** is a broker who is employed to negotiate a transaction between both parties and who for that purpose may be an agent of both parties, acting fairly so as not to favor one party over the other.

Agency Relationships

Agent (Broker)	Principal (Client)	Third Party (Customer)
Seller's Agent	Seller	Buyer
Subagent	Seller	Buyer
Buyer's Agent	Buyer	Seller
Intermediary	Buyer and Seller	None

Seller's Agent

A **seller's agent** is a broker who obtains a listing from a seller to act as an agent for compensation. The seller's agent is often referred to as the **listing agent** or seller's broker. A **listing agreement** is an employment contract between an owner of real property and broker for the sale of real estate. A seller's agent has a fiduciary duty to get the seller the maximum amount a "ready, willing, and able" buyer will pay, with the terms most favorable to the seller.

Subagent

A **subagent** is a broker who accepts an offer of subagency offered by the listing agent. Therefore, subagents take on the same fiduciary duties as primary agents. The subagent represents the seller and has the buyer as a customer. If the selling agent is a subagent for the seller, then the selling agent owes a fiduciary duty and loyalty to the seller.

Buyer's Agent

A **buyer's agent** is a broker employed by the buyer to locate a certain kind of real property. A buyer's agent has a fiduciary duty to get his or her client or principal, the best possible price, and terms in the acquisition of the property. The buyer's agent is a single agency relationship.

Selling Agent

A **selling agent** is the broker who presents an offer to purchase from a "ready, willing, and able buyer". Since a selling agent finds the buyer, an issue that can be confusing is the question of whether the selling agent represents the seller or the buyer. Buyers commonly believe that the selling agent represents the buyer. Others assume that the selling agent is a subagent of the listing broker and represents the seller. This is best addressed through obtaining a "buyer's representation" agreement, which is an employment contract outlining the terms of the relationship.

Most property is sold through a local association of brokers called a multiple listing service. A **multiple listing service (MLS)** is a cooperative listing service conducted by a group of brokers, usually members of a real estate association. Listings are submitted to a central bureau where they are entered into a computerized system and printed regularly in a multiple listing book that is available to the members. The MLS maintains an inventory of all the available, listed properties in the area. Any MLS member may view the listed properties and obtain offers from buyers for these properties even though he or she is not the listing broker.

Nothing in the listing agreement compels the selling agent to represent the seller. The listing agreement is an employment contract exclusively between the seller and the listing broker. Thus, a selling agent does not automatically become a subagent when he or she shows a listed property. As long as complete disclosure is made about agency relationships, the selling agent can represent either the seller or the buyer.

Selling agents should choose to be either the seller's agent or the buyer's agent, and make sure their actions conform to their choice. They should be aware of the practical and legal consequences of this choice to avoid a conflict of loyalties.

In general, if the selling agent is acting like the agent of the buyer, he or she is the agent of the buyer. An agency relationship is created between the broker and the buyer by implication. The buyer becomes the selling agent's principal, and the seller becomes the **third party**. It is safe to assume that the agency relationship starts as soon as the selling agent begins acting in the best interest of the buyer.

Intermediary

A broker may represent both parties in the real estate transaction as an intermediary. The intermediary role was created to provide brokers with a way to represent both parties to a transaction and avoid the numerous pitfalls of dual agency.

A written employment contract, signed and agreed to by both the buyer and seller, is mandatory for an intermediary relationship to exist. In an intermediary relationship, the broker works with both the buyer and seller, and must act fairly, not favoring one party over the other.

Permission for an intermediary relationship is addressed in the listing agreement of MLS contracts; therefore, there is no need to address this again upon receipt of a contract.

A broker who has no associates, who does not receive approval from the buyer and seller to relinquish his or her fiduciary duties, may not act as an intermediary. He or she must either assign or allow one of the parties to the transaction to obtain representation from another broker, or offer to appoint each party one of his or her associates, who would be able to provide advice and opinion with full fiduciary duties.

Remember, fiduciary duties include confidentiality without expiration; therefore, information received by the agent that could affect a real estate transaction may never be disclosed, unless written permission has been obtained. That is, intermediary allows the broker's appointed associates to provide the opinions and advice to their respective principals. The broker cannot directly advise or represent the seller or potential buyer.

Nevertheless, the establishment of intermediary status requires several procedural steps. If the broker or broker's associates fail to meet any of the required steps adequately, then the intermediary status and all of the benefits associated with it will be void.

Step One

If the buyer submits an offer, the offer must include a request for approval of an intermediary relationship.

Step Two

Upon approval of the seller and buyer of an intermediary relationship, the broker will either:

- proceed with the negotiations, with the broker working "with" both parties (similar to a customer relationship).
- appoint an associate to represent the buyer and seller, with each receiving the advice and opinions of their respective associates.

A broker or his or her associate **cannot**:

- divulge that the seller will accept a lower price than the listing price.
- divulge that a buyer will pay more than a submitted written offer.
- discuss information that either party has specified as confidential.

Review - Agency
- In a real estate transaction, the agent is always a broker.
- In a listing agreement, the agent of the seller (principal) is the listing agent (broker) or seller's agent.
- In a listing agreement, a subagent represents the seller.
- In a listing agreement, a broker who represents and works for both buyer and seller is an intermediary.
- In a buyer representation agreement, the agent of the buyer is the buyer's agent or buyer broker.

Agents Working for Broker

A **sales associate** (also called an **associate licensee**) is a licensed real estate salesperson or broker whose license is held by a sponsoring licensed broker. The sales associate works for a sponsoring broker, and the sponsoring broker is responsible for the acts of the sales associate. A sales associate is the agent of his or her sponsoring broker and must deal fairly with the broker's customers. Sales associates are not agents of the buyer or seller in a real property transaction, even though a buyer or seller may refer to the salesperson as "my agent". Because there is a general agency relationship between the broker and the associate, the broker is bound by the acts of the associate, provided they are within the realm of his or her real estate related activities.

> Example: Rose, a sales associate in the employ of broker Dan, listed a property owned by Miranda. Under the law, the agency has been created between Miranda and broker Dan. Rose is bound by the agency because she represents Dan.

Disclosing Agency Relationship

Traditionally, the principal in a real estate transaction was a seller, represented by the listing broker. The selling broker might have represented the principal as a subagent. Then, as now, the selling broker was legally bound by a fiduciary duty to the seller. So who represented the buyer when the listing broker wrote up the offer? Who represented the buyer when a selling broker wrote up the offer and presented it to the seller? The answer is—no one. Legally, the buyer had no representation, even though it appeared to be the licensed agent showing the property and writing up the offer.

The requirement to disclose agency and reveal what relationship the parties have with each other came out of public demand for assurance of representation in all real estate dealings.

Agency Disclosure Process

In 1995, the Texas legislature created a uniform process regarding The Real Estate License Act, resulting in two rules: (1) Initial Meetings and (2) Representation.

1. Initial Meetings

This rule provides that at the first meeting or substantive dialogue with a party, a licensee must furnish the party with an Information About Brokerage Services form (Form OP-K).

Substantive dialogue is defined as a substantive conversation or written correspondence regarding a specific property. Substantive communications do not include an open house for prospective purchasers or tenants or communications that transpire after the parties to a transaction have signed a contract to buy, sell, lease, or rent.

Licensees are not required to provide an Information About Brokerage Services if acting as an agent for a lease less than one year in length with no future sales considerations, or if the party the licensee meets is already represented by another licensee.

2. Representation

Agency disclosure rules require that a licensee who represents a party in a real estate transaction must disclose this relationship to any other party involved in the transaction and any other licensee who represents a party to the transaction. This disclosure must take place at first contact and may be oral or in writing. Of course, common business practice suggests that it be done in writing, with the licensee retaining a signed copy of the form.

Creating Agency Relationship

An agency relationship may be created between an agent and principal by **agreement**, **ratification**, or **estoppel**. It is created by an express or implied, written or oral contract. Brokers are fiduciaries whether the agency is created by oral agreement or by express (written) agreement.

Review - Creating an Agency Relationship
- Agreement
- Ratification
- Estoppel (Ostensible or Implied Agency)

Agency by Agreement

An agency relationship may be created by agreement, also known as **express agency**, with or without a written contract. However, a real estate agreement must be in writing to be enforceable in a court of law. The two common ways to create agency with a written real estate contract are through a listing agreement or a buyer representation agreement.

Listing Agreements

A **listing agreement** is a written contract by which a principal, or seller, employs a broker to sell real estate. When the seller signs a listing agreement promising payment for service by the listing broker and the broker promises to "use due diligence" in finding a buyer, it is a **bilateral contract**—in that a promise is given in exchange for a promise.

Review – A listing agreement is the most common way to create an agency relationship.

The listing agreement occurs when the seller promises to pay a commission upon presentation of a "ready, willing, and able" buyer who meets all the terms of the listing. A **"ready, willing, and able"** buyer is one who is prepared to enter into a purchase contract, is ready to buy, and meets the financing requirements of purchase. A listing agreement gives the broker the right to be paid only after doing the job, or producing results. Think of it as simply an employment contract between the seller and the broker.

Under agency law, the listing broker is a **special agent** who deals in the name of the principal to negotiate the sale of property. The broker does not have control over the property itself, while acting within the course of a special agency, but only has the right to represent that principal. The seller is not promising to sell the house, nor can the seller be forced to sell even after signing a listing agreement. The seller is promising to pay a commission to the broker if he or she brings a "ready, willing, and able" buyer.

> Example: Ellen, a licensed real estate broker, spoke to everyone in her area at least once a month. Since she was well known, when owners wanted to sell their homes, they called Ellen. She met with the owners to complete the listing agreement. An agency by express, written agreement was created.

Buyer Representation Agreements

As single agency becomes more prevalent, more brokers represent the buyer to locate a property rather than represent the seller. Typically, an agency relationship is created through the Buyer/Tenant Representation Agreement – Residential. The listing agreement is to the seller as the buyer representation agreement is to the buyer. As with all exclusive agreements, a definite termination date is specified. Also, the manner of the broker's compensation is described, stating that all real estate commissions are negotiable.

Agency by Ratification

Ratification means acceptance of an act already performed. Ratification of an agency relationship is created by approving acts after they are done. For example, a seller can accept an offer presented by a licensee and agree to pay a commission, even though no agency has been approved. The seller creates an agency by ratification by accepting the actions of the agent after the fact.

> Example: As Ellen walked through the neighborhood talking to people, she became familiar with most of the homes in the area. One day, she answered the office phone and talked to a caller who described the type of home he wanted to buy. She knew of one just like his description, but it was not listed for sale. She called the owner of the house, who told her she could show it to the prospective buyer. Afterward, she presented an offer from the buyer that included a request to pay Ellen a commission. The owner accepted the offer and agreed to pay Ellen a commission, creating an agency by ratification.

Agency by Estoppel

Finally, an agency relationship can be created by estoppel. **Estoppel** is a legal bar that prevents a person from asserting facts or rights that are not consistent with what was implied by the person's previous behavior. That is why this is also called an **implied** or **ostensible** (apparent) agency. Agency is created when the principal causes a third party to believe another person is the principal's agent. What the principal has implied by his or her behavior is barred, or stopped, from being denied. Authority is given when a principal allows a third party to believe that another person is the agent, even if the third party is unaware of the appointment.

> Example: If a seller allows a buyer to believe a broker represents the seller, and the buyer believes that to be so, the existence of an agency cannot be denied by the seller, who will be bound by the actions of the broker. This is known as the Doctrine of Estoppel.

Ostensible or Implied Agency

A licensee must be aware that an agency relationship can result from his or her conduct, even though no express employment contract has been signed, or possible payments established. This is a subject where great care must be taken to assure that the agent is operating correctly under the law.

When a broker takes a listing, he or she promises to represent the seller while finding a buyer. The broker has a **fiduciary** duty to conduct negotiations in the best interest of the seller in dealing with buyers who are interested in the property. However, in Texas, the distinction of who represents whom can be blurred unintentionally.

As the seller's agent, a broker has the duty of utmost care, integrity, honesty, and loyalty when dealing with the seller. Yet the law also requires the broker to exercise reasonable skill and care, engage in honest and fair dealing, and fully disclose all material facts to all parties. It is difficult for an agent to live up to his or her fiduciary duty to a seller and at the same time meet general obligations to a buyer. Some services may be offered to a buyer without creating an ostensible or implied agency of the buyer.

Seller's Agent or Subagent May:
- Show the buyer properties meeting the buyer's requirements and describe to the buyer a property's amenities, attributes, condition, and status;
- Complete a standard purchase contract by inserting the terms of the buyer's offer in the form's blanks and transmit all offers of the buyer to the seller on a timely basis;
- Inform the buyer about the availability of financing, legal service, inspection companies, title companies, or other related services desired or required by the buyer to complete the transaction.

While performing the above tasks, it is very difficult not to establish an implied agency with the buyer. A seller's agent must be extremely alert and conscious of his or her role at all times to avoid creating an intermediary relationship by implication or conduct.

Listing brokers would violate their agency relationships with their sellers if they made the following types of comments to buyers.

Avoid Comments Like These

- "Leave it all up to me. I can get you the house at the price you want."
- "I am sure I can get the seller to agree to this price and get the financing you need."
- "I know the seller personally, and I am sure they will not counter at that price."
- "The house has been for sale for more than eight months and I think it is listed too high. Let's make a lower offer to see if they take it."
- "If the sellers insist on their asking price, I will remind them that the heating system is old; the carpet is not exactly designer quality; and the whole place needs repainting. That should convince them to reduce their price."
- "I will write up the offer for you and present it to the seller. If they do not like it, I can always try to find out their bottom line and we can go from there."

Terminating Agency Relationship

At any time during the agency, the principal or agent may terminate the agency, except in an agency coupled with an interest. An **agency coupled with an interest** is one in which the agent gets an interest in the subject of the agency (the property). For example, a broker might advance funds to pay for a defaulted loan on the property to keep it out of foreclosure. The seller cannot revoke the listing after the broker has cured the loan.

When May An Agency Be Terminated?

- Full performance of its terms
- Expiration of its term
- Agreement of the parties
- Acts of the parties
- Destruction of the property
- Death, incapacity, or insanity of the broker or principal
- Bankruptcy of the principal

Since the relationship between a principal and agent is a personal one, the principal has the right to revoke the agency at any time. If the cancellation is without good reason, the seller may be liable for breach of contract and may be liable to pay a commission to the listing broker.

An agency agreement must be in writing for the agent to enforce a commission claim based upon a breach of contract.

Summary

Agency is a legal relationship in which a principal authorizes an agent to act as the principal's representative when dealing with third parties. Most agency relationships have a **principal**, an **agent**, and a **third party**. In a real estate transaction the principal (buyer or seller), agent (real estate broker), and third party (customer) are bound together in a legal relationship, with all the duties and rights that go with that connection. When a broker represents only the buyer or the seller in the transaction, it is called **single agency**. Different agency relationships include the **listing agent**, the **subagent**, the **buyer's agent**, the **dual agent** (not allowed in Texas), an **intermediary**, a **selling agent**, and a **sales associate** who works for the broker.

In 1995, the Texas legislature created a uniform process regarding The Real Estate License Act, resulting in two rules: **Initial Meetings** and **Representation**.

A real estate agency can be created by **express agreement**, **ratification**, and **estoppel**. Usually an agency relationship is created by a listing contract between the seller and broker. A contract between a broker and a buyer is called the **buyer representation agreement**.

Termination of agency can be made at any time by the principal or the agent, unless it is an agency **coupled with an interest**. Agency may also be terminated by expiration of terms, full performance of terms, destruction of the property, or death or incapacity of either principal or agent.

Unit 4

Listing Agreements

Introduction

The listing agreement outlines the terms and provisions in a sales listing for real property. It is essentially an employment contract between a seller and a real estate broker. A real estate salesperson should become an expert in the different types of listing agreements, and understand the mechanics of each, so that he or she may explain them to clients.

Learning Objectives

After reading this unit, you should be able to:

- explain different types of listing agreements.
- determine commissions under various listing agreements.
- explain an exclusive right to sell form.

Types of Listing Agreements

Now that you understand the concept of an agency relationship, the next step is to look closely at one of the most commonly used real estate contract forms - the **listing agreement**. This agreement represents the creation of an agency relationship between a real estate broker and a seller. The different types of listing agreements are the open listing, the net listing, the exclusive agency listing, and most commonly, the exclusive right to sell listing.

Open Listing

In an **open listing**, the seller may employ as many brokers as needed to sell the property. The seller is obligated to pay a commission only to the broker responsible for bringing a "ready, willing, and able" buyer. However, if the seller is able to find a buyer due to his or her own efforts, the seller is not obligated to pay the broker a commission.

Net Listing

A **net listing** is a type of listing agreement where the difference between the actual sales price and the seller's desired sales price determines the broker's commission. If a seller desires to sell his or her property for $100,000 and the broker sells it for $105,000, the broker's commission would be $5000 ($105,000 minus $100,000). This scenario presents an advantage to the broker since he or she can use due diligence to find the highest price possible, which would result in a higher commission. This practice, however, may lead to an unscrupulous broker turning down lower offers in order to achieve a higher commission. To prevent this, the listing agreement should specify a maximum price, which would limit the broker's commission.

Exclusive Agency Listing

In an **exclusive agency listing**, only one broker has authorization to list the property for sale and obtain a buyer. If a salesperson from another brokerage finds a buyer for the property, the original broker specified in the exclusive agency listing agreement is entitled to the commission. However, the seller also has the authority to find a buyer on his or her own. If the seller is the procuring cause for the sale, the broker will not be entitled to a commission. The **procuring cause** is the effort that brings about the desired result.

Exclusive Right to Sell Listing

An **exclusive right to sell listing** is the most desirable type of listing agreement from the broker's point of view. It specifies that regardless of who is the procuring cause for the sale, the listing broker is entitled to a commission. That broker is the exclusive agent of the seller. Therefore, if the property owner or another agent finds a buyer, the named broker must receive the commission. This listing agreement is the most popular among brokers. It contains a beginning date and a definite termination date. The terms and provisions of this type of listing agreement are found in an exclusive right to sell form.

Exclusive Right to Sell Form

The **Residential Real Estate Listing Agreement - Exclusive Right to Sell** form is commonly used when one real estate broker agrees to market a seller's property for a certain period of time, with specific terms and a specified price. The form is promulgated by the Texas Association of REALTORS® (TAR), and the blanks are to be completed by the licensee.

RESIDENTIAL REAL ESTATE LISTING AGREEMENT
EXCLUSIVE RIGHT TO SELL

1. **PARTIES:** The parties to this agreement (this Listing) are:

   Seller: _____
   _____
   Address: _____
   City, State, Zip: _____
   Phone: _____ Fax: _____
   E-Mail: _____

   Broker: _____
   Address: _____
   City, State, Zip: _____
   Phone: _____ Fax: _____
   E-Mail: _____

   Seller appoints Broker as Seller's sole and exclusive real estate agent and grants to Broker the exclusive right to sell the Property.

2. **PROPERTY:** "Property" means the land, improvements, and accessories described below, except for any described exclusions.

   A. <u>Land:</u> Lot _____ , Block _____ , _____
   _____ Addition, City of _____ ,
   in _____ County, Texas known as _____
   _____ (address/zip code),
   or as described on attached exhibit. *(If Property is a condominium, attach Condominium Addendum.)*

   B. <u>Improvements:</u> The house, garage and all other fixtures and improvements attached to the above-described real property, including without limitation, the following **permanently installed and built-in items**, if any: all equipment and appliances, valances, screens, shutters, awnings, wall-to-wall carpeting, mirrors, ceiling fans, attic fans, mail boxes, television antennas and satellite dish system and equipment, heating and air-conditioning units, security and fire detection equipment, wiring, plumbing and lighting fixtures, chandeliers, water softener system, kitchen equipment, garage door openers, cleaning equipment, shrubbery, landscaping, outdoor cooking equipment, and all other property owned by Seller and attached to the above-described real property.

   C. <u>Accessories:</u> The following described related accessories, if any: window air conditioning units, stove, fireplace screens, curtains and rods, blinds, window shades, draperies and rods, controls for satellite dish system, controls for garage door openers, entry gate controls, door keys, mailbox keys, above-ground pool, swimming pool equipment and maintenance accessories, and artificial fireplace logs.

   D. <u>Exclusions:</u> The following improvements and accessories will be retained by Seller and must be removed prior to delivery of possession: _____ .

   E. <u>Owners' Association:</u> The property ☐ is ☐ is not subject to mandatory membership in a property owners' association.

(TAR-1101) 7-16-08   Initialed for Identification by Broker/Associate _____ and Seller _____ , _____   Page 1 of 8

Residential Listing concerning _____

3. **LISTING PRICE:** Seller instructs Broker to market the Property at the following price: $ _____
    (Listing Price). Seller agrees to sell the Property for the Listing Price or any other price acceptable to Seller. Seller will pay all typical closing costs charged to sellers of residential real estate in Texas (seller's typical closing costs are those set forth in the residential contract forms promulgated by the Texas Real Estate Commission).

4. **TERM:**

    A. This Listing begins on _____ and ends at 11:59 p.m. on _____ .

    B. If Seller enters into a binding written contract to sell the Property before the date this Listing begins and the contract is binding on the date this Listing begins, this Listing will not commence and will be void.

5. **BROKER'S FEE:**

    A. <u>Fee</u>: When earned and payable, Seller will pay Broker a fee of:

    ☐ (1) _____ % of the sales price.

    ☐ (2) _____

    B. <u>Earned</u>: Broker's fee is earned when any one of the following occurs during this Listing:
        (1) Seller sells, exchanges, options, agrees to sell, agrees to exchange, or agrees to option the Property to anyone at any price on any terms;
        (2) Broker individually or in cooperation with another broker procures a buyer ready, willing, and able to buy the Property at the Listing Price or at any other price acceptable to Seller; or
        (3) Seller breaches this Listing.

    C. <u>Payable</u>: Once earned, Broker's fee is payable either during this Listing or after it ends at the earlier of:
        (1) the closing and funding of any sale or exchange of all or part of the Property;
        (2) Seller's refusal to sell the Property after Broker's Fee has been earned;
        (3) Seller's breach of this Listing; or
        (4) at such time as otherwise set forth in this Listing.

        Broker's fee is <u>not</u> payable if a sale of the Property does not close or fund as a result of: (i) Seller's failure, without fault of Seller, to deliver to a buyer a deed or a title policy as required by the contract to sell; (ii) loss of ownership due to foreclosure or other legal proceeding; or (iii) Seller's failure to restore the Property, as a result of a casualty loss, to its previous condition by the closing date set forth in a contract for the sale of the Property.

    D. <u>Other Fees</u>:

        (1) <u>Breach by Buyer Under a Contract</u>: If Seller collects earnest money, the sales price, or damages by suit, compromise, settlement, or otherwise from a buyer who breaches a contract for the sale of the Property entered into during this Listing, Seller will pay Broker, after deducting attorney's fees and collection expenses, an amount equal to the lesser of one-half of the amount collected after deductions or the amount of the Broker's Fee stated in Paragraph 5A. Any amount paid under this Paragraph 5D(1) is in addition to any amount that Broker may be entitled to receive for subsequently selling the Property.

        (2) <u>Service Providers</u>: If Broker refers Seller or a prospective buyer to a service provider (for example, mover, cable company, telecommunications provider, utility, or contractor) Broker may receive a fee from the service provider for the referral. Any referral fee Broker receives under this Paragraph 5D(2) is in addition to any other compensation Broker may receive under this Listing.

(TAR-1101) 7-16-08   Initialed for Identification by Broker/Associate _____ and Seller _____ , _____   Page 2 of 8

Residential Listing concerning _____

    (3) <u>Transaction Fees or Reimbursable Expenses</u>: _____
_____
_____ .

E. <u>Protection Period</u>:

    (1) "Protection period" means that time starting the day after this Listing ends and continuing for _____ days. "Sell" means any transfer of any interest in the Property whether by oral or written agreement or option.

    (2) Not later than 10 days after this Listing ends, Broker may send Seller written notice specifying the names of persons whose attention was called to the Property during this Listing. If Seller agrees to sell the Property during the protection period to a person named in the notice or to a relative of a person named in the notice, Seller will pay Broker, upon the closing of the sale, the amount Broker would have been entitled to receive if this Listing were still in effect.

    (3) This Paragraph 5E survives termination of this Listing. This Paragraph 5E will not apply if:
      (a) Seller agrees to sell the Property during the protection period;
      (b) the Property is exclusively listed with another broker who is a member of the Texas Association of REALTORS® at the time the sale is negotiated; and
      (c) Seller is obligated to pay the other broker a fee for the sale.

F. <u>County</u>: All amounts payable to Broker are to be paid in cash in _____
_____ County, Texas.

G. <u>Escrow Authorization</u>: Seller authorizes, and Broker may so instruct, any escrow or closing agent authorized to close a transaction for the purchase or acquisition of the Property to collect and disburse to Broker all amounts payable to Broker under this Listing.

6. LISTING SERVICES:

❏ A. Broker will file this Listing with one or more Multiple Listing Services (MLS) by the earlier of the time required by MLS rules or 5 days after the date this Listing begins. Seller authorizes Broker to submit information about this Listing and the sale of the Property to the MLS.

    <u>Notice</u>: MLS rules require Broker to accurately and timely submit all information the MLS requires for participation including sold data. Subscribers to the MLS may use the information for market evaluation or appraisal purposes. Subscribers are other brokers and other real estate professionals such as appraisers and may include the appraisal district. Any information filed with the MLS becomes the property of the MLS for all purposes. **Submission of information to MLS ensures that persons who use and benefit from the MLS also contribute information.**

❏ B. Broker will not file this Listing with a Multiple Listing Service (MLS) or any other listing service.

7. ACCESS TO THE PROPERTY:

A. <u>Authorizing Access</u>: Authorizing access to the Property means giving permission to another person to enter the Property, disclosing to the other person any security codes necessary to enter the Property, and lending a key to the other person to enter the Property, directly or through a keybox. To facilitate the showing and sale of the Property, Seller instructs Broker to:
    (1) access the Property at reasonable times
    (2) authorize other brokers, their associates, inspectors, appraisers, and contractors to access the Property at reasonable times; and
    (3) duplicate keys to facilitate convenient and efficient showings of the Property.

B. <u>Scheduling Companies</u>: Broker may engage the following companies to schedule appointments and to authorize others to access the Property: _____ .

(TAR-1101) 7-16-08   Initialed for Identification by Broker/Associate _____ and Seller _____ . _____   Page 3 of 8

Residential Listing concerning _____

C. <u>Keybox</u>: A keybox is a locked container placed on the Property that holds a key to the Property. A keybox makes it more convenient for brokers, their associates, inspectors, appraisers, and contractors to show, inspect, or repair the Property. The keybox is opened by a special combination, key, or programmed device so that authorized persons may enter the Property, even in Seller's absence. Using a keybox will probably increase the number of showings, but involves risks (for example, unauthorized entry, theft, property damage, or personal injury). Neither the Association of REALTORS® nor MLS requires the use of a keybox.

(1) Broker ❏ is ❏ is not   authorized to place a keybox on the Property.

(2) If a tenant occupies the Property at any time during this Listing, Seller will furnish Broker a written statement (for example, TAR No. 1411), signed by all tenants, authorizing the use of a keybox or Broker may remove the keybox from the Property.

D. <u>Liability and Indemnification</u>: When authorizing access to the Property, Broker, other brokers, their associates, any keybox provider, or any scheduling company are not responsible for personal injury or property loss to Seller or any other person. Seller assumes all risk of any loss, damage, or injury. **Except for a loss caused by Broker, Seller will indemnify and hold Broker harmless from any claim for personal injury, property damage, or other loss.**

8. **COOPERATION WITH OTHER BROKERS:** Broker will allow other brokers to show the Property to prospective buyers. Broker will offer to pay the other broker a fee as described below if the other broker procures a buyer that purchases the Property.

A. <u>MLS Participants</u>: If the other broker is a participant in the MLS in which this Listing is filed, Broker will offer to pay the other broker:
(1) if the other broker represents the buyer: _____ % of the sales price or $ _____ ; and
(2) if the other broker is a subagent: _____ % of the sales price or $ _____ .

B. <u>Non-MLS Brokers</u>: If the other broker is not a participant in the MLS in which this Listing is filed, Broker will offer to pay the other broker:
(1) if the other broker represents the buyer: _____ % of the sales price or $ _____ ; and
(2) if the other broker is a subagent: _____ % of the sales price or $ _____ .

9. **INTERMEDIARY:** *(Check A or B only.)*

❏ A. <u>Intermediary Status</u>: Broker may show the Property to interested prospective buyers who Broker represents. If a prospective buyer who Broker represents offers to buy the Property, Seller authorizes Broker to act as an intermediary and Broker will notify Seller that Broker will service the parties in accordance with one of the following alternatives.

(1) If a prospective buyer who Broker represents is serviced by an associate other than the associate servicing Seller under this Listing, Broker may notify Seller that Broker will: (a) appoint the associate then servicing Seller to communicate with, carry out instructions of, and provide opinions and advice during negotiations to Seller; and (b) appoint the associate then servicing the prospective buyer to the prospective buyer for the same purpose.

(2) If a prospective buyer who Broker represents is serviced by the same associate who is servicing Seller, Broker may notify Seller that Broker will: (a) appoint another associate to communicate with, carry out instructions of, and provide opinions and advice during negotiations to the prospective buyer; and (b) appoint the associate servicing the Seller under this Listing to the Seller for the same purpose.

(3) Broker may notify Seller that Broker will make no appointments as described under this Paragraph 9A and, in such an event, the associate servicing the parties will act solely as Broker's intermediary representative, who may facilitate the transaction but will not render opinions or advice during negotiations to either party.

(TAR-1101) 7-16-08   Initialed for Identification by Broker/Associate _____ and Seller _____ , _____   Page 4 of 8

Residential Listing concerning _____

☐ B. <u>No Intermediary Status</u>: Seller agrees that Broker will not show the Property to prospective buyers who Broker represents.

Notice: If Broker acts as an intermediary under Paragraph 9A, Broker and Broker's associates:
- may not disclose to the prospective buyer that Seller will accept a price less than the asking price unless otherwise instructed in a separate writing by Seller;
- may not disclose to Seller that the prospective buyer will pay a price greater than the price submitted in a written offer to Seller unless otherwise instructed in a separate writing by the prospective buyer;
- may not disclose any confidential information or any information Seller or the prospective buyer specifically instructs Broker in writing not to disclose unless otherwise instructed in a separate writing by the respective party or required to disclose the information by the Real Estate License Act or a court order or if the information materially relates to the condition of the property;
- may not treat a party to the transaction dishonestly; and
- may not violate the Real Estate License Act.

10. **CONFIDENTIAL INFORMATION:** During this Listing or after it ends, Broker may not knowingly disclose information obtained in confidence from Seller except as authorized by Seller or required by law. Broker may not disclose to Seller any confidential information regarding any other person Broker represents or previously represented except as required by law.

11. **BROKER'S AUTHORITY:**

A. Broker will use reasonable efforts and act diligently to market the Property for sale, procure a buyer, and negotiate the sale of the Property.

B. In addition to other authority granted by this Listing, Broker may:
   (1) advertise the Property by means and methods as Broker determines, including but not limited to creating and placing advertisements with interior and exterior photographic and audio-visual images of the Property and related information in any media and the Internet;
   (2) place a "For Sale" sign on the Property and remove all other signs offering the Property for sale or lease;
   (3) furnish comparative marketing and sales information about other properties to prospective buyers;
   (4) disseminate information about the Property to other brokers and to prospective buyers, including applicable disclosures or notices that Seller is required to make under law or a contract;
   (5) obtain information from any holder of a note secured by a lien on the Property;
   (6) accept and deposit earnest money in trust in accordance with a contract for the sale of the Property;
   (7) disclose the sales price and terms of sale to other brokers, appraisers, or other real estate professionals;
   (8) in response to inquiries from prospective buyers and other brokers, disclose whether the Seller is considering more than one offer, provided that Broker will not disclose the terms of any competing offer unless specifically instructed by Seller;
   (9) advertise, during or after this Listing ends, that Broker "sold" the Property; and
   (10) place information about this Listing, the Property, and a transaction for the Property on an electronic transaction platform (typically an Internet-based system where professionals related to the transaction such as title companies, lenders, and others may receive, view, and input information).

C. Broker is not authorized to execute any document in the name of or on behalf of Seller concerning the Property.

(TAR-1101) 7-16-08   Initialed for Identification by Broker/Associate _____ and Seller _____ , _____   Page 5 of 8

Residential Listing concerning _____

12. **SELLER'S REPRESENTATIONS:** Except as provided by Paragraph 15, Seller represents that:
   A. Seller has fee simple title to and peaceable possession of the Property and all its improvements and fixtures, unless rented, and the legal capacity to convey the Property;
   B. Seller is not bound by a listing agreement with another broker for the sale, exchange, or lease of the Property that is or will be in effect during this Listing;
   C. any pool or spa and any required enclosures, fences, gates, and latches comply with all applicable laws and ordinances;
   D. no person or entity has any right to purchase, lease, or acquire the Property by an option, right of refusal, or other agreement;
   E. there are no delinquencies or defaults under any deed of trust, mortgage, or other encumbrance on the Property;
   F. the Property is not subject to the jurisdiction of any court;
   G. all information relating to the Property Seller provides to Broker is true and correct to the best of Seller's knowledge; and
   H. the name of any employer, relocation company, or other entity that provides benefits to Seller when selling the Property is: _____ .

13. **SELLER'S ADDITIONAL PROMISES:** Seller agrees to:
   A. cooperate with Broker to facilitate the showing, marketing, and sale of the Property;
   B. not rent or lease the Property during this Listing without Broker's prior written approval;
   C. not negotiate with any prospective buyer who may contact Seller directly, but refer all prospective buyers to Broker;
   D. not enter into a listing agreement with another broker for the sale, exchange, or lease of the Property to become effective during this Listing;
   E. maintain any pool and all required enclosures in compliance with all applicable laws and ordinances;
   F. provide Broker with copies of any leases or rental agreements pertaining to the Property and advise Broker of tenants moving in or out of the Property;
   G. complete any disclosures or notices required by law or a contract to sell the Property; and
   H. amend any applicable notices and disclosures if any material change occurs during this Listing.

14. **LIMITATION OF LIABILITY:**

   A. If the Property is or becomes vacant during this Listing, Seller must notify Seller's casualty insurance company and request a "vacancy clause" to cover the Property. Broker is not responsible for the security of the Property nor for inspecting the Property on any periodic basis.

   B. **Broker is not responsible or liable in any manner for personal injury to any person or for loss or damage to any person's real or personal property resulting from any act or omission not caused by Broker's negligence, including but not limited to injuries or damages caused by:**
      (1) other brokers, their associates, inspectors, appraisers, and contractors who are authorized to access the Property;
      (2) acts of third parties (for example, vandalism or theft);
      (3) freezing water pipes;
      (4) a dangerous condition on the Property; or
      (5) the Property's non-compliance with any law or ordinance.

   C. **Seller agrees to protect, defend, indemnify, and hold Broker harmless from any damage, costs, attorney's fees, and expenses that:**
      (1) are caused by Seller, negligently or otherwise;
      (2) arise from Seller's failure to disclose any material or relevant information about the Property; or
      (3) are caused by Seller giving incorrect information to any person.

(TAR-1101) 7-16-08   Initialed for Identification by Broker/Associate _____ and Seller _____ , _____   Page 6 of 8

Residential Listing concerning _____

15. SPECIAL PROVISIONS:

16. DEFAULT: If Seller breaches this Listing, Seller is in default and will be liable to Broker for the amount of the Broker's fee specified in Paragraph 5A and any other fees Broker is entitled to receive under this Listing. If a sales price is not determinable in the event of an exchange or breach of this Listing, the Listing Price will be the sales price for purposes of computing Broker's fee. If Broker breaches this Listing, Broker is in default and Seller may exercise any remedy at law.

17. MEDIATION: The parties agree to negotiate in good faith in an effort to resolve any dispute related to this Listing that may arise between the parties. If the dispute cannot be resolved by negotiation, the dispute will be submitted to mediation. The parties to the dispute will choose a mutually acceptable mediator and will share the cost of mediation equally.

18. ATTORNEY'S FEES: If Seller or Broker is a prevailing party in any legal proceeding brought as a result of a dispute under this Listing or any transaction related to or contemplated by this Listing, such party will be entitled to recover from the non-prevailing party all costs of such proceeding and reasonable attorney's fees.

19. ADDENDA AND OTHER DOCUMENTS: Addenda that are part of this Listing and other documents that Seller may need to provide are:
- ✓ A. Information About Brokerage Services;
- ❏ B. Seller Disclosure Notice (§5.008, Texas Property Code);
- ❏ C. Seller's Disclosure of Information on Lead-Based Paint and Lead-Based Paint Hazards (required if Property was built before 1978);
- ❏ D. Residential Real Property Affidavit (T-47 Affidavit; related to existing survey);
- ❏ E. MUD, Water District, or Statutory Tax District Disclosure Notice (Chapter 49, Texas Water Code);
- ❏ F. Request for Information from an Owners' Association;
- ❏ G. Request for Mortgage Information;
- ❏ H. Information about Mineral Clauses in Contract Forms;
- ❏ I. Information about On-Site Sewer Facility;
- ❏ J. Information about Property Insurance for a Buyer or Seller;
- ❏ K. Information about Special Flood Hazard Areas;
- ❏ L. Condominium Addendum to Listing;
- ❏ M. Keybox Authorization by Tenant;
- ❏ N. Seller's Authorization to Release and Advertise Certain Information; and
- ❏ O. _____

20. AGREEMENT OF PARTIES:

A. <u>Entire Agreement</u>: This Listing is the entire agreement of the parties and may not be changed except by written agreement.

B. <u>Assignability</u>: Neither party may assign this Listing without the written consent of the other party.

(TAR-1101) 7-16-08   Initialed for Identification by Broker/Associate _____ and Seller _____ , _____   Page 7 of 8

Residential Listing concerning _____

   C. <u>Binding Effect</u>: Seller's obligation to pay Broker an earned fee is binding upon Seller and Seller's heirs, administrators, executors, successors, and permitted assignees.

   D. <u>Joint and Several</u>: All Sellers executing this Listing are jointly and severally liable for the performance of all its terms.

   E. <u>Governing Law</u>: Texas law governs the interpretation, validity, performance, and enforcement of this Listing.

   F. <u>Severability</u>: If a court finds any clause in this Listing invalid or unenforceable, the remainder of this Listing will not be affected and all other provisions of this Listing will remain valid and enforceable.

   G. <u>Notices</u>: Notices between the parties must be in writing and are effective when sent to the receiving party's address, fax, or e-mail address specified in Paragraph 1.

21. ADDITIONAL NOTICES:

   A. Broker's fees or the sharing of fees between brokers are not fixed, controlled, recommended, suggested, or maintained by the Association of REALTORS®, MLS, or any listing service.

   B. Fair housing laws require the Property to be shown and made available to all persons without regard to race, color, religion, national origin, sex, disability, or familial status. Local ordinances may provide for additional protected classes (for example, creed, status as a student, marital status, sexual orientation, or age).

   C. Seller may review the information Broker submits to an MLS or other listing service.

   D. Broker advises Seller to remove or secure jewelry, prescription drugs, and other valuables.

   E. Statutes or ordinances may regulate certain items on the Property (for example, swimming pools and septic systems). Non-compliance with the statutes or ordinances may delay a transaction and may result in fines, penalties, and liability to Seller.

   F. If the Property was built before 1978, Federal law requires the Seller to: (1) provide the buyer with the federally approved pamphlet on lead poisoning prevention; (2) disclose the presence of any known lead-based paint or lead-based paint hazards in the Property; (3) deliver all records and reports to the buyer related to such paint or hazards; and (4) provide the buyer a period up to 10 days to have the Property inspected for such paint or hazards.

   G. Broker cannot give legal advice. READ THIS LISTING CAREFULLY. If you do not understand the effect of this Listing, consult an attorney BEFORE signing.

Broker's Printed Name	License No.	Seller	Date
By: _____		_____	
Broker's Associate's Signature	Date	Seller	Date

(TAR-1101) 7-16-08

The sections below are found in the Residential Real Estate Listing Agreement - Exclusive Right to Sell form.

1. Parties

Section 1 of the Exclusive Right to Sell contract requires all parties to the agreement to be identified, including you and your client (the seller). The blank lines ask for both parties' full names; addresses; city, state, and zip code; phone number; fax number; and e-mail address.

Exercise care when entering information in this section. Be sure to include the full legal name of each party, as well as complete addresses with suite or apartment numbers if applicable.

The bottom line of Section 1 clearly states the intention of the parties signing the contract - the seller is appointing the broker as his or her sole and exclusive agent to sell the property.

2. Property

Section 2 of the Listing Agreement calls for the property to be identified. The information required in this section differs slightly from the information required in the Purchase Agreement. The Listing Agreement asks for the property's street address and legal description, as well as the city, county, and zip code.

Carefully complete this section because incorrect property information could render the listing agreement unenforceable.

Section 2B and 2C list the improvements and accessories included, without limitation, in the listing. If the seller decides to keep any fixtures or accessories, Section 2D provides space for the seller to list those items. Section 2E identifies if a property contains common use areas and is subject to an owner's association.

3. Listing Price

Determining the correct price is crucial. The listing price is a key factor that determines whether a property will sell. The seller instructs the broker to market the property at a specific price (listing price), which is written in the appropriate blank. In addition, the seller hereby agrees to sell the property for the indicated listing price or any other acceptable price, and will pay all closing costs typically charged to the seller.

4. Term

Section 4 identifies the term of duration for the listing. The paragraph provides a blank space for the date the listing begins, and the date the listing ends, at 11:59 p.m. If the seller enters into a binding agreement to sell the property before the listing agreement begins, the listing agreement becomes void.

5. Broker's Fee

As shown in section 5, the broker may be paid a percentage of the sales price or through a method specified in the blank space provided, such as a flat fee. In a typical listing agreement, real estate licensees are paid 6% of the sales price, but this is negotiable with the seller.

The broker earns a fee when the:

- seller sells, exchanges, options, agrees to sell, agrees to exchange, or agrees to option the property.
- broker procures a "ready, willing, and able" buyer.
- seller breaches the terms of the listing agreement.

Once the broker has earned a fee, it is payable when:

- there is a closing and funding of any sale or exchange of the property.
- the seller refuses to sell the property after the broker's fee has been rightfully earned.
- the seller breaches the terms of the listing agreement.
- some other time is specified in the listing agreement.

The broker's fee is not payable if the:

- property does not sell because the seller failed to deliver a title policy to the buyer.
- seller loses the property through foreclosure or other legal proceedings.
- seller fails to restore the property to its previous condition by the closing date established in the purchase agreement in the event the property is damaged through casualty loss.

Section 5D specifies other fees that may be paid and under what circumstances. For example, if a buyer enters into a purchase agreement with the seller and then breaches the contract, the broker is eligible for one-half of the amount stated in Section 5A. If the seller collects the amount of the sales price from a buyer who breached the contract, the broker is due one-half of the fee listed in Section 5A.

Section 5E addresses the **protection period** or the period of time starting the day after the listing agreement expires and lasting for a specified number of days. The protection period prevents a broker from losing his or her fee to a seller who does not want to pay it and simply waits until the listing agreement expires. For example, if the seller then agrees to sell the property during the protection period to a buyer who was known during the listing period, the broker is due the amount he or she would have earned had the property closed during the listing period.

Section 5E survives the termination of the listing agreement. However, it will not apply if the seller agrees to sell the property during the protection period and the property is listed with another broker at the time the sale is negotiated.

Section 5F specifies that any fees paid to the broker must be paid in cash in a specified county in Texas. Section 5G states that the seller authorizes and the broker can instruct any escrow or closing agent to collect and disburse all due fees to the broker.

6. Listing Services

Section 6 of the listing agreement indicates if the listing will be filed with a Multiple Listing Service. If the listing is to be filed with one or more Multiple Listing Services, the broker agrees to file the listing within five days after the date the listing begins, or as the MLS requires, whichever is earlier. By agreeing to file with a Multiple Listing Service, the seller allows more exposure of the property to other brokers, which may result in a quicker sale.

7. Access to the Property

Section 7 authorizes certain people to access the property, and specifies how they will have access. A person is authorized to have access to the property by the disclosure of access codes and lending a key directly to the person or through a lockbox. A lockbox is especially helpful when time constraints are a factor in showing property. A lockbox allows access to the property while the seller is away, resulting in more exposure to prospective buyers and possibly a faster sale. For example, a lockbox may be beneficial if a seller is at work during the weekdays and only available during weekends to show the property. The seller instructs the broker and the broker's associates to access the property at reasonable times, and authorizes the brokers, inspectors, appraisers, and contractors to access the property at reasonable times.

In Section 7C, the seller gives or retains permission for the broker to place a **keybox** on the property to facilitate access. A keybox is a container that holds the key to the property so that real estate brokers, salespersons, and other service professionals can access the property in the seller's absence. Opening the keybox requires a special combination or key in order to limit access to authorized individuals. Brokers, associates, or scheduling companies are not responsible for personal injury or property loss to the seller if the seller authorizes access to the property.

8. Cooperation with Other Brokers

Section 8 specifies that the broker will allow other brokers to show the property to prospective buyers. If another broker procures an acceptable offer, the broker pays the other broker part of the broker's fee if the other broker represents the buyer. In a typical 6% commission agreement, the listing broker will retain 3.5% while the buyer's broker receives 2.5%. Another common arrangement is 3% and 3%. This section will also specify commission splits for members and non-members of a Multiple Listing Service.

9. Intermediary

Section 9 outlines the agency relationship that exists between the broker and the seller of the property in the event that a prospective buyer is represented by the same broker. The two options are intermediary status or no intermediary status. An **intermediary** is a broker who has been authorized in writing by the parties to a purchase agreement to represent both parties following statutory provisions defined in Section 1101.559 of the Texas Real Estate Act.

Intermediary status allows the broker to represent a prospective buyer and the seller with or without appointments. If appointments are acceptable, and the prospective buyer is represented by a different associate broker than the broker who represents the seller, the broker appoints the associate servicing the seller to carry out instructions and provide opinions and advice to only the seller. The broker also instructs the associate servicing the prospective buyer to do the same for the buyer.

If the prospective buyer and seller are serviced by the same associate, the broker must notify the seller that the broker will assign another associate to work with the prospective buyer; or the broker will make no appointments to either party and the associate who was servicing both parties will act only as the broker's intermediary representative. This means the associate facilitates the transaction, but must not give any opinions or advice to either party during negotiations.

If a broker acts as an intermediary, the broker and any of the broker's associates:

- may not disclose to the prospective buyer that the seller will accept a price less than the asking price unless the seller instructs the broker to do so in writing.

- may not disclose to the seller that a prospective buyer will pay a greater price than the listing price, unless specifically authorized in writing by the buyer.

- may not disclose any confidential information unless otherwise authorized by the respective party or if required by The Real Estate License Act (TRELA).

- must treat all parties to the transaction honestly.

- will comply with TRELA.

If the seller opts for no intermediary status:

- the seller does not want the broker to show the property to any prospective buyers that the broker represents.

- the broker will exclusively represent the seller and no prospective buyers.

10. Confidential Information

Section 10 does not require the broker or seller to complete any blanks or check any boxes. It simply expresses that the broker cannot knowingly disclose any information obtained in confidence from the seller unless specifically authorized by the seller or required by law. The broker cannot disclose to the seller any confidential information about any other person the broker represents or has represented in the past, unless required by law.

11. Broker's Authority

Section 11 outlines the **broker's authority**, which is to make reasonable efforts and act diligently to sell the property. The broker cannot execute any document in the name of, or on behalf of, the seller.

The broker may:

- advertise the property in any media the broker decides, including the newspapers, magazine ads, and the Internet.

- place interior and exterior photos of the property in any advertising media, including the Internet.

- place a "For Sale" sign on the property and remove any other signs on the property offering it for sale or lease.

- furnish comparative marketing and sales information about other properties to prospective buyers.

- provide information about the property to other brokers and prospective buyers.

- obtain information from a holder of a note secured by a lien on the property.

- accept and deposit earnest money in trust as part of a contract for sale of the property.

- disclose the sales price and terms of the sale to other brokers and real estate salespeople.

- advertise the property as "sold" during or after the listing ends.

- place information about the listing on an electronic platform (an Internet-based information system used by real estate salespeople related to the transaction to receive, view, and input information).

12. Seller's Representations

In Section 12, the seller assures that he or she has a fee simple title to and possession of the property and all its fixtures and has the legal capacity to convey the property. In addition, the seller also represents that he or she is not bound by a listing agreement with a different broker for the sale, exchange, or lease of this property that will be in effect at the time of this listing agreement. Any pool or spa, required enclosures, fences, gates, and latches comply with applicable laws and ordinances. No person has the right to purchase, lease, or acquire the property by an option, right of refusal, or other agreement; and there are no delinquencies or defaults under a deed of trust, mortgage, or other encumbrances on the property.

The seller also represents that the property is not subject to the jurisdiction of any court; and all information relating to the property that the seller provides to the broker is true and correct. Finally, the seller must provide the name of any employer, relocation company, or other entity that provides benefits to the seller, as well as how the seller learned of the broker's firm.

13. Seller's Additional Promises

Section 13 lists any additional promises made by the seller when signing the listing agreement.

The seller promises:

A. to cooperate with the broker to facilitate the showing and marketing of the property. This may include allowing the property to be shown at open houses, having a "For Sale" sign posted on the property, and listing of the property on an MLS Website.

B. not to rent or lease the property during listing without the broker's prior written approval. Encumbering the property with a renter or lessor may complicate the transfer of property and negotiations.

C. not to negotiate with any prospective buyer who may contact the seller directly, but instead refer all prospective buyers to the broker. The seller must not attempt to negotiate the sale of his or her property outside the broker and the listing contract. During the listing period, the broker is the only one who may negotiate directly with a prospective buyer.

D. not to enter into a listing agreement with another broker for the sale, exchange, or lease of the property to become effective during this listing. Only the listing broker can enter into an agreement for the sale, exchange, or lease of the property during the listing period.

E. to maintain any pool and all required enclosures in compliance with all applicable laws and ordinances. The property owner must maintain the property according to local laws during the listing period.

F. to provide the broker with copies of any leases or rental agreements pertaining to the property and advise the broker of tenants moving in or out of the property. The broker must be aware of any existing and current encumbrances affecting the property and any tenants occupying the property.

G. to complete any disclosures or notices required by law or a contract to sell the property. The seller must disclose any pertinent information about the property.

H. to amend any applicable notices and disclosures if any material change occurs during this listing. If the seller submits a disclosure at the beginning of the listing, but then the condition of the property changes, the seller must update the disclosure to reflect the property's current state.

14. Limitation of Liability

The seller and broker are responsible for certain conditions and situations, but their liability is limited. This section outlines those limitations. Section 14A requires the seller to notify his or her casualty insurance company in the event that the property is or becomes vacated during the listing period. The seller must request a **vacancy clause**, which allows an insurance company to provide coverage for a property while it is vacant. The broker is not responsible for the security of the property or for inspecting the property during the listing period.

Section 14B states that the broker is not responsible or liable for the personal injury, loss, or damage to any person's personal property due to an act or omission not caused by the broker's negligence.

The broker is not liable for:

1. other broker's inspectors, appraisers, and contractors who are authorized to access the property.

2. acts of third parties (for example, vandalism or theft).
3. freezing water pipes.
4. a dangerous condition on the property.
5. the property's non-compliance with any law or ordinance.

Section 14C states that the seller agrees to protect, defend, indemnify, and hold the broker harmless from any damages, costs, attorney's fees, and expenses:

1. for which the broker is not responsible under the listing.
2. that arise from the seller's failure to disclose any material or relevant information about the property.
3. that are caused by the seller giving incorrect information to broker, other brokers, or prospective buyers.

15. Special Provisions

Section 15 is simply a blank space where the broker may fill in any special provisions that are included as part of the listing agreement.

16. Default

Section 16 specifies the penalties faced by the seller if he or she defaults on the listing contract. Among other things, the seller may breach the contract by leasing or selling the property without the broker's prior consent. If the seller does breach the contract, the seller is liable to the broker for the amount of the broker's fee and any other fees the broker may be entitled to. If the sales price is not determinable because the property was exchanged or the listing agreement was breached, to compute the broker's fee, the listing price will be the sales price. However, if the broker breaches the listing agreement, the seller may exercise any remedy allowable by law.

17. Mediation

A dispute between a seller and a broker that cannot be reconciled often requires mediation. Section 17 states that the parties to the listing agreement agree to negotiate in good faith when trying to resolve a dispute that may arise related to the listing. The parties to the listing will choose the mediator and will share the cost of mediation equally.

18. Attorney's Fees

Section 18 specifies that if a legal proceeding is brought to resolve a dispute between the parties to the listing contract, or any transaction related to or contemplated by the listing agreement, the non-prevailing party must pay the other party the costs of the proceeding and reasonable attorneys' fees.

19. Addenda and Other Documents

Section 19 provides an opportunity for the broker to disclose any addenda, disclosures, or additional documents that are part of the listing and that the seller needs to provide.

These documents include:

a.   Information About Brokerage Services.

b.   Seller's Disclosure Notice (5.008, Texas Property Code).

c.   Seller's Disclosure of Information on Lead-Based Paint and Lead-Based Paint Hazard (if property was built before 1978).

d.   MUD Disclosure Notice (Chapter 49, Texas Water Code).

e.   request for information from an owner's association.

f.   request for mortgage information.

g.   information about on-site sewer facility.

h.   information about special flood hazard areas.

i.   condominium addendum.

j.   keybox authorization by tenant.

k.   Seller's Authorization to Release and Advertise Certain Information.

l.   the last option is a blank line to be completed by the broker if necessary.

20. Agreement of Parties

Section 20 has no blank lines or boxes to be completed by the broker. Instead, Section 20 is a list of the statements and concepts the parties to the listing contract agree to by signing the document.

Agreement of the Parties

a.   The parties fully agree to the listing and it may not be changed except by written agreement.

b.   The listing contract may not be assigned unless the other party provides his or her written consent.

c.   The seller's obligation to pay the broker's fee is binding for the seller, seller's heirs, administrators, executors, successors, and permitted assignees.

d.   All sellers entering into the listing agreement are jointly and severally liable for the performance of all the terms of the listing.

e.   The listing contract's interpretation, validity, performance, and enforcement are subject to Texas law.

f. If a court finds any clause in the listing invalid or unenforceable, the rest of the contract will not be affected and the remaining sections are still enforceable and valid.

g. Any notices must be sent to the parties.

21. Additional Notices

Section 21, the final section of the listing contract, provides additional important information about the agreement, relevant laws, and terms.

Important Information

a. The broker's fees are not fixed, controlled, recommended, suggested, or maintained by the Association of REALTORS®, MLS, or any other listing service.

b. The property is subject to fair housing laws and must be shown and made available to all persons without regard to race, color, religion, national origin, sex, disability, or familial status. Local ordinances may provide additional protection.

c. The seller has the right to review any information the broker submits to the MLS or other listing service.

d. The seller is advised to secure and/or remove valuable personal property from the property.

e. The property must comply with statues and ordinances; failure to do so may delay the transaction and result in fines, penalties, and liability to the seller.

f. Residential service companies may provide service contracts to repair or replace appliances or electrical, plumbing, heating, or cooling systems.

g. The broker may not give legal advice. The seller is advised to consult an attorney before signing the contract if he or she does not fully understand the terms or information.

The listing agreement is complete with the signature of the broker and the seller and their respective Social Security or Tax ID numbers.

Summary

One of the most common contracts a real estate salesperson will encounter is the **listing agreement**. The agreement outlines the terms and provisions in a sales listing for real property. A real estate salesperson should become an expert in the different types of listing agreements, and understand the mechanics of each, so that he or she is able to explain them to the client. The different types of listing agreements are the **open listing**, the **net listing**, the **exclusive agency listing**, and most commonly, the **exclusive right to sell listing**. An exclusive right to sell listing is the most desirable type of listing agreement from the broker's point of view.

It specifies that regardless of who is the procuring cause for the sale, the listing broker is entitled to a commission.

The **Residential Real Estate Listing Agreement - Exclusive Right to Sell** form is commonly used in Texas when one real estate broker agrees to market a seller's property for a certain period of time, with specific terms and a specified price. The form is available from the Texas Association of REALTORS® (TAR) and the blanks are to be completed by the licensee. You should complete all of the sections of the form carefully and be able to explain each section to the seller.

Unit 5
Buyer Representation Agreement

Introduction

Now that you understand a listing agreement on the seller's side, you will learn about the buyer's side of the transaction. Buying real estate is one of the largest purchases most consumers make in their lifetime. While some buyers navigate through the complicated world of real estate on their own, most require the resources of an agent to simplify the process. A buyer needs agent representation just as a seller does to guide them through the purchase of real property. As you learned in Unit 3, a **buyer's agent** is a broker employed by the buyer to locate real property. This agency relationship is created through the Residential Buyer/Tenant Representation Agreement (typically known as the Buyer Representation Agreement). This unit discusses the agreement and explains each section.

Learning Objectives

After reading this unit, you should be able to:

- discuss the need for buyer representation.
- identify the need for a buyer representation agreement.
- list the sections of the Buyer Representation Agreement.
- explain each section of Buyer Representation Agreement.

Buyer Representation

Traditionally, no one had a clear legal responsibility to act in the buyer's interest in a real estate sale. However, as buyers became more knowledgeable, single agency became more common and more brokers represented and protected the interests of buyers.

Typically, a buyer representation agreement is used to create an agency relationship. This agreement is to a buyer what a listing agreement is to a seller. As with all exclusive agreements, a definite termination date is specified. The manner of the broker's compensation is also described.

During the course of their career, many salespeople alternate between representing a seller when listing a property and representing a buyer when showing a property. It is important to remember who represents whom in a real estate transaction.

If a buyer works exclusively with a broker or sales associate, the broker or sales associate must first present a written disclosure regarding the agency relationship before entering into an agreement. If the buyer does not work with the sales associate or broker exclusively, the selling agent (who may also be the listing agent) must provide a written disclosure regarding the agency relationship before the buyer makes an offer to purchase. A buyer representation agreement is the written disclosure that expresses this agency relationship.

Residential Buyer/Tenant Representation Agreement

In a real estate transaction in Texas, the **Residential Buyer/Tenant Representation Agreement** is the common contract form that defines the working relationship between a buyer and the buyer's agent and creates an agency relationship. Another variation of the form exists for someone interested in purchasing commercial property, but the Residential Buyer/Tenant Representation Agreement refers only to residential property. This Buyer Representation Agreement may also apply to prospective tenants who would like to occupy rental property. The Texas Association of REALTORS® creates the form. The Buyer Representation Agreement entitles the real estate broker to a commission if the broker finds real property for the buyer, or if the buyer finds the property on his or her own.

TEXAS ASSOCIATION OF REALTORS®
RESIDENTIAL BUYER/TENANT REPRESENTATION AGREEMENT
USE OF THIS FORM BY PERSONS WHO ARE NOT MEMBERS OF THE TEXAS ASSOCIATION OF REALTORS® IS NOT AUTHORIZED.
©Texas Association of REALTORS®, Inc. 2006

1. **PARTIES:** The parties to this agreement are:

Client: _____
_____
    Address: _____
    City, State, Zip: _____
    Phone:_____Fax: _____
    E-Mail: _____

Broker: _____
    Address: _____
    City, State, Zip: _____
    Phone:_____Fax: _____
    E-Mail: _____

2. **APPOINTMENT:** Client grants to Broker the exclusive right to act as Client's real estate agent for the purpose of acquiring property in the market area.

3. **DEFINITIONS:**
A. *"Acquire"* means to purchase or lease.
B. *"Closing"* in a sale transaction means the date legal title to a property is conveyed to a purchaser of property under a contract to buy. "Closing" in a lease transaction means the date a landlord and tenant enter into a binding lease of a property.
C. *"Market area"* means that area in the State of Texas within the perimeter boundaries of the following areas:_____
_____
_____
_____.
D. *"Property"* means any interest in real estate including but not limited to properties listed in a multiple listing service or other listing services, properties for sale by owners, and properties for sale by builders.

4. **TERM:** This agreement commences on _____ and ends at 11:59 p.m. on _____.

5. **BROKER'S OBLIGATIONS:** Broker will: (a) use Broker's best efforts to assist Client in acquiring property in the market area; (b) assist Client in negotiating the acquisition of property in the market area; and (c) comply with other provisions of this agreement.

6. **CLIENT'S OBLIGATIONS:** Client will: (a) work exclusively through Broker in acquiring property in the market area and negotiate the acquisition of property in the market area only through Broker; (b) inform other brokers, salespersons, sellers, and landlords with whom Client may have contact that Broker exclusively represents Client for the purpose of acquiring property in the market area and refer all such persons to Broker; and (c) comply with other provisions of this agreement.

7. **REPRESENTATIONS:**
A. Each person signing this agreement represents that the person has the legal capacity and authority to bind the respective party to this agreement.
B. Client represents that Client is not now a party to another buyer or tenant representation agreement with another broker for the acquisition of property in the market area.

(TAR-1501) 4-14-06   Initialed for Identification by: Broker/Associate _____, and Client _____, _____   Page 1 of 4

Buyer/Tenant Representation Agreement between _____

    C. Client represents that all information relating to Client's ability to acquire property in the market area Client gives to Broker is true and correct.

    D. Name any employer, relocation company, or other entity that will provide benefits to Client when acquiring property in the market area: _____.

8. INTERMEDIARY: *(Check A or B only.)*

❑ A. <u>Intermediary Status</u>: Client desires to see Broker's listings. If Client wishes to acquire one of Broker's listings, Client authorizes Broker to act as an intermediary and Broker will notify Client that Broker will service the parties in accordance with one of the following alternativ es.

    (1) If the owner of the property is serviced by an associate other than the associate servicing Client under this agreement, Broker may notify Client that Broker will: (a) appoint the associate then servicing the owner to communicate with, carry out instructions of, and provide opinions and advice during negotiations to the owner; and (b) appoint the associate then servicing Client to the Client for the same purpose.

    (2) If the owner of the property is serviced by the same associate who is servicing Client, Broker may notify Client that Broker will: (a) appoint another associate to communicate with, carry out instructions of, and provide opinions and advice during negotiations to Client; and (b) appoint the associate servicing the owner under the listing to the owner for the same purpose.

    (3) Broker may notify Client that Broker will make no appointments as described under this Paragraph 8A and, in such an event, the associate servicing the parties will act solely as Broker's intermediary representative, who may facilitate the transaction but will not render opinions or advice during negotiations to either party.

❑ B. <u>No Intermediary Status</u>: Client does not wish to be shown or acquire any of Broker's listings.

Notice: **If Broker acts as an intermediary under Paragraph 8A, Broker and Broker's associates:**

    ♦ **may not disclose to Client that the seller or landlord will accept a price less than the asking price unless otherwise instructed in a separate writing by the seller or landlord;**

    ♦ **may not disclose to the seller or landlord that Client will pay a price greater than the price submitted in a written offer to the seller or landlord unless otherwise instructed in a separate writing by Client;**

    ♦ **may not disclose any confidential information or any information a seller or landlord or Client specifically instructs Broker in writing not to disclose unless otherwise instructed in a separate writing by the respective party or required to disclose the information by the Real Estate License Act or a court order or if the information materially relates to the condition of the property;**

    ♦ **shall treat all parties to the transaction honestly; and**

    ♦ **shall comply with the Real Estate License Act.**

9. COMPETING CLIENTS:

Client acknowledges that Broker may represent other prospective buyers or tenants who may seek to acquire properties that may be of interest to Client. Client agrees that Broker may, during the term of this agreement and after it ends, represent such other prospects, show the other prospects the same properties that Broker shows to Client, and act as a real estate broker for such other prospects in negotiating the acquisition of properties that Client may seek to acquire.

10. CONFIDENTIAL INFORMATION:

    A. During the term of this agreement or after its termination, Broker may not knowingly disclose information obtained in confidence from Client except as authorized by Client or required by law. Broker may not disclose to Client any information obtained in confidence regarding any other person Broker represents or may have represented except as required by law.

    B. Unless otherwise agreed or required by law, a seller or the seller's agent is not obliged to keep the existence of an offer or its terms confidential. If a listing agent receives multiple offers, the listing agent is obliged to treat the competing buyers fairly.

(TAR-1501) 4-14-06   Initialed for Identification by: Broker/Associate _____, and Client _____, _____   Page 2 of 4

Buyer/Tenant Representation Agreement between _____

11. BROKER'S FEES:

A. <u>Commission</u>: The parties agree that Broker will receive a commission calculated as follows: (1) ____% of the gross sales price if Client agrees to purchase property in the market area; and (2) if Client agrees to lease property in the market a fee equal to *(check only one box)*: ❏ _____% of one month's rent or ❏ ____% of all rents to be paid over the term of the lease.

B. <u>Source of Commission Payment</u>: Broker will seek to obtain payment of the commission specified in Paragraph 11A first from the seller, landlord, or their agents. If such persons refuse or fail to pay Broker the amount specified, Client will pay Broker the amount specified less any amounts Broker receives from such persons.

C. <u>Earned and Payable</u>: A person is not obligated to pay Broker a commission until such time as Broker's commission is *earned and payable*. Broker's commission is *earned* when: (1) Client enters into a contract to buy or lease property in the market area; or (2) Client breaches this agreement. Broker's commission is *payable*, either during the term of this agreement or after it ends, upon the earlier of: (1) the closing of the transaction to acquire the property; (2) Client's breach of a contract to buy or lease a property in the market area; or (3) Client's breach of this agreement. If Client acquires more than one property under this agreement, Broker's commissions for each property acquired are earned as each property is acquired and are payable at the closing of each acquisition.

D. <u>Additional Compensation</u>: If a seller, landlord, or their agents offer compensation in excess of the amount stated in Paragraph 11A (including but not limited to marketing incentives or bonuses to cooperating brokers) Broker may retain the additional compensation in addition to the specified commission. Client is not obligated to pay any such additional compensation to Broker.

E. <u>Acquisition of Broker's Listing</u>: Notwithstanding any provision to the contrary, if Client acquires a property listed by Broker, Broker will be paid in accordance with the terms of Broker's listing agreement with the owner and Client will have no obligation to pay Broker.

F. In addition to the commission specified under Paragraph 11A, Broker is entitled to the following fees.
   (1) <u>Construction</u>: If Client uses Broker's services to procure or negotiate the construction of improvements to property that Client owns or may acquire, Client ensures that Broker will receive from Client or the contractor(s) at the time the construction is substantially complete a fee equal to:
   _____.
   (2) <u>Service Providers</u>: If Broker refers Client or any party to a transaction contemplated by this agreement to a service provider (for example, mover, cable company, telecommunications provider, utility, or contractor) Broker may receive a fee from the service provider for the referral.
   (3) <u>Other</u>: _____
   _____
   _____

G. <u>Protection Period</u>: "Protection period" means that time starting the day after this agreement ends and continuing for _____ days. Not later than 10 days after this agreement ends, Broker may send Client written notice identifying the properties called to Client's attention during this agreement. If Client or a relative of Client agrees to acquire a property identified in the notice during the protection period, Client will pay Broker, upon closing, the amount Broker would have been entitled to receive if this agreement were still in effect. This Paragraph 11G survives termination of this agreement. This Paragraph 11G will not apply if Client is, during the protection period, bound under a representation agreement with another broker who is a member of the Texas Association of REALTORS® at the time the acquisition is negotiated and the other broker is paid a fee for negotiating the transaction.

H. <u>Escrow Authorization</u>: Client authorizes, and Broker may so instruct, any escrow or closing agent authorized to close a transaction for the acquisition of property contemplated by this agreement to collect and disburse to Broker all amounts payable to Broker.

I. <u>County</u>: Amounts payable to Broker are to be paid in cash in _____ County, Texas.

(TAR-1501) 4-14-06   Initialed for Identification by: Broker/Associate _____, and Client _____, _____   Page 3 of 4

Buyer/Tenant Representation Agreement between _____

12. MEDIATION: The parties agree to negotiate in good faith in an effort to resolve any dispute that may arise related to this agreement or any transaction related to or contemplated by this agreement. If the dispute cannot be resolved by negotiation, the parties will submit the dispute to mediation before resorting to arbitration or litigation and will equally share the costs of a mutually acceptable mediator.

13. DEFAULT: If either party fails to comply with this agreement or makes a false representation in this agreement, the non-complying party is in default. If Client is in default, Client will be liable for the amount of compensation that Broker would have received under this agreement if Client was not in default. If Broker is in default, Client may exercise any remedy at law.

14. ATTORNEY'S FEES: If Client or Broker is a prevailing party in any legal proceeding brought as a result of a dispute under this agreement or any transaction related to this agreement, such party will be entitled to recover from the non-prevailing party all costs of such proceeding and reasonable attorney's fees.

15. LIMITATION OF LIABILITY: Neither Broker nor any other broker, or their associates, is responsible or liable for Client's personal injuries or for any loss or damage to Client's property that is not caused by Broker. Client will hold broker, any other broker, and their associates, harmless from any such injuries or losses. Client will indemnify Broker against any claims for injury or damage that Client may cause to others or their property.

16. ADDENDA: Addenda and other related documents which are part of this agreement are:
- ☑ Information About Brokerage Services
- ❑ Protecting Your Home from Mold
- ❑ Information Concerning Property Insurance
- ❑ General Information and Notice to a Buyer
- ❑ Protect Your Family from Lead in Your Home
- ❑ Information about Special Flood Hazard Areas
- ❑ For Your Protection: Get a Home Inspection
- ❑ _____

17. SPECIAL PROVISIONS:

18. ADDITIONAL NOTICES:

A. Broker's fees and the sharing of fees between brokers are not fixed, controlled, recommended, suggested, or maintained by the Association of REALTORS® or any listing service.

B. Broker's services are provided without regard to race, color, religion, national origin, sex, disability or familial status.

C. Broker is not a property inspector, surveyor, engineer, environmental assessor, or compliance inspector. Client should seek experts to render such services in any acquisition.

D. If Client purchases property, Client should have an abstract covering the property examined by an attorney of Client's selection, or Client should be furnished with or obtain a title policy.

E. Buyer may purchase a residential service contract. Buyer should review such service contract for the scope of coverage, exclusions, and limitations. The purchase of a residential service contract is optional. There are several residential service companies operating in Texas.

F. Broker cannot give legal advice. This is a legally binding agreement. READ IT CAREFULLY. If you do not understand the effect of this agreement, consult your attorney BEFORE signing.

Broker's Printed Name _____ License No. _____ Client _____ Date

By:_____

Broker's Associate's Signature Date   Client _____ Date

(TAR-1501) 4-14-06

Page 4 of 4

In the following discussion, we will refer to the Residential Buyer/Tenant Representation Agreement as the Buyer Representation Agreement. The following sections are found in the Buyer Representation Agreement.

1. Parties

Section 1 of the Buyer Representation Agreement contract requires all parties to the agreement to be identified, including the buyer and the broker. There are blank lines available that will contain the names of the buyer and broker along with the following contact information: addresses including the city, state, and zip code; phone number; fax number; and e-mail addresses. When filling out the agreement, make sure the information in this section is accurate and correct.

2. Appointment

Section 2 of the Buyer Representation Agreement includes an appointment statement. An **appointment statement** is a clause stating that the buyer exclusively grants the broker the authority to act as his or her agent with the sole purpose of locating real property to purchase. The appointment statement summarizes the fiduciary duty that the broker owes to the buyer. Section 5 of this agreement describes the full scope of the broker's fiduciary duties.

3. Definitions

At times, the terminology used in a contract can be vague or seem to convey different meanings, which may cause the parties confusion. Section 3 defines the terminology used in the agreement. This prevents the parties from interpreting the agreement incorrectly and reduces possible ambiguity. As a licensee, you should refer to these definitions when they appear elsewhere in the representation agreement. In the agreement, **acquire** means to purchase or lease real property. **Closing** refers to the date that title will transfer to the purchaser. **Market area** is the area in Texas within the boundaries of specified areas listed in the contract. **Property** refers to any interest in real estate that includes, but is not limited to properties in a multiple listing service, for sale by owner properties, and properties for sale by builders.

4. Term

Section 4 identifies the term, or duration of, the Buyer Representation Agreement. The paragraph provides a blank space for the date the agency relationship begins and the date it ends. The agreement expires at 11:59 p.m. on the specified date or the closing date of the transaction for the acquired property. The term of the representation agreement is negotiable between the buyer and the broker.

TEXAS LAW OF CONTRACTS

5. Broker's Obligations

By agreeing to the Buyer Representation Agreement, the broker must fulfill the fiduciary duties owed to the buyer. According to Section 5, the broker has the following obligations:

A. The broker must do everything in his or her power to help the buyer purchase real property in the area specified in Section 3.

B. After a suitable property is located in the specified market area, the broker must help the client in the negotiation process of acquiring the property.

C. Along with the above duties, the broker must also comply with any other provisions within the Buyer Representation Agreement.

6. Client's Obligations

While the broker has certain duties to fulfill for the buyer, the buyer also owes the broker certain obligations under this agreement. Section 6 indicates that the client must comply with the following:

A. The buyer is obligated to work only with the broker exclusively in purchasing property in the market area. The buyer cannot collude with another broker in the purchase and negotiation of acquiring property.

B. In the search for real property, it is likely that the buyer may encounter other parties besides their broker. However, under the provisions of this agreement, the buyer must make other parties aware that they are under exclusive representation from a broker.

C. Just as the broker must do in Section 5, the buyer must comply with any other specified provisions in this agreement.

7. Representations

Section 7 lists certain representations that the parties must make under this agreement.

A. The parties signing this agreement must have both the mental capacity and the legal authority to bind them to this contract.

B. The buyer must enter the contract without having current representation from another broker.

C. The buyer must also provide accurate information as to his or her ability to acquire real property in the specified market area.

D. If the buyer is obtaining assistance to acquire real property from an entity other than the broker, they must disclose that party in the blank space provided.

8. Intermediary

Section 8 of the Buyer Representation Agreement states that the broker will exclusively represent the buyer in acquiring property other than those listed by the broker. However, this does not prevent the buyer from purchasing any listed properties from the broker. For such properties, the buyer can choose to consent to the following agency relationships in this section.

A. Intermediary Status

If the buyer is interested in viewing the broker's listings, the buyer authorizes the broker to act as an intermediary in the sales transaction. An intermediary is a broker who works with both the buyer and seller, and must act fairly, not favoring one party over the other. If this is the case, the buyer has the option of either allowing or disallowing appointments.

If the buyer allows the possibility of appointments, then the broker has the authority to appoint the associate licensee under the listing agreement to assist with the acquisition of the property. However, the associate licensee in the listing agreement must also continue to service the owner of the property. If the buyer is interested in one of the broker's listed properties that involve the same associate licensee under the Buyer Representation Agreement, the broker has two options. He or she can either appoint a different licensee to service the owner under the listing agreement or have the associate licensee under the Buyer Representation Agreement act for both parties. Either way, the broker must notify the client of his or her decisions in handling the transaction.

If the buyer does not wish to allow appointments, then the broker will not appoint specific associate licensees to either the buyer or the seller. The licensees servicing the buyer and seller will become intermediary representatives of the broker and not influence the decisions of either party.

B. No Intermediary Status

If the buyer is not interested in viewing the broker's listings, then no intermediary status by the broker is necessary. A special notice at the end of this section addresses the broker acting as an intermediary.

The broker and the broker's associate:

- may not disclose to the prospective buyer that the seller or landlord will accept a price less than the asking price unless the seller or landlord instructs the broker to do so in writing.

- may not disclose to the seller that a prospective buyer will pay a greater price than the listing price, unless specifically authorized in writing by the buyer.

- may not disclose any confidential information unless otherwise authorized by the respective party or if required by the TRELA.
- must treat all parties to the transaction honestly.
- will comply with the TRELA.

9. Competing Clients

According to Section 9 of the Buyer Representation Agreement, the buyer must acknowledge that the broker has the authority to enter into similar agreements with **competing clients** or other buyers represented by the same broker. Therefore, the broker can show other prospective buyers the same properties during the duration of the representation agreement. More exposure to a property will increase the likelihood of a buyer being interested in purchasing the property. Brokers owe a fiduciary duty to competing clients and should treat them equally when showing them the same property.

10. Confidential Information

This section expresses that the broker cannot knowingly disclose any information obtained in confidence from the buyer unless he or she is specifically authorized by the buyer or required by law. Failure to maintain confidentiality of the buyer may constitute a violation of the broker's fiduciary duty. The broker cannot disclose to the buyer any confidential information about any other person the broker represents or has represented in the past, unless required by law. In addition, sellers or their agents cannot keep an existing offer confidential and must treat competing buyers fairly.

11. Broker's Fees

This section explains how to handle the payment for the broker's commission.

A. This section specifies how the commission will be paid to the broker. The broker can obtain a commission via a percentage of the sales price or a percentage of the monthly rental if it is a lease.

B. The broker is entitled to payment of a commission from the seller, landlord, or his or her respective agents. If any of the parties fail to pay the amount specified in Section A, the buyer will pay that amount minus any amounts paid by the parties mentioned in this section.

C. A broker's commission is earned when one of the following occurs:

- the buyer enters into a sales contract.
- the buyer defaults on the Buyer Representation Agreement.

A broker's commission is payable when one of the following occurs:

- the sales transaction closes and the buyer acquires the property.
- the buyer defaults on the sales contract.
- the buyer defaults on the Buyer Representation Agreement.

D. The broker can receive additional compensation from sellers, landlords, or his or her agents through marketing incentives or bonuses through cooperating brokers.

E. If the buyer acquires a property listed by the broker, the fees paid are outlined in the broker's listing agreement with the property owner.

F. The broker can earn additional fees if he or she helps procure construction improvements to the property acquired or if the broker refers the buyer to a service provider. A blank space is left for any extra fees that the broker may receive.

G. This section details the protection period for the broker's commission. The protection period begins the day after the Buyer Representation Agreement ends and continues for the specified number of days in this section. The **protection period (Agreement)** is a clause that entitles a broker to a commission if the buyer acquires property that was called to the buyer's attention during the duration of the agreement. However, the protection period will not apply if the buyer enters into another Buyer Representation Agreement with another broker.

H. The buyer and the broker both authorize the escrow agent handling the transaction to collect and disburse any amounts payable to the broker.

I. This section specifies the Texas county where the broker commission will be paid.

12. Mediation

Section 12 states that the parties to the Buyer Representation Agreement agree to negotiate in good faith when trying to resolve any dispute that may arise due to events related to the agreement. If the negotiations fail and the parties cannot come to an agreement, the dispute will be settled by mediation. The parties to the agreement will choose the mediator and split the cost of mediation equally.

13. Default

This section identifies the actions of the buyer or broker that would qualify for default of the agreement. If either party does not comply with the provisions of the agreement or makes some type of misrepresentation, then they are in default of the contract. The broker in the agreement may receive his or her proposed commission payment if the buyer defaults. On the other hand, the buyer has the right to exercise remedies at law if the broker defaults on the agreement.

14. Attorney's Fees

If legal intervention is required to settle a dispute between the parties of the agreement, the non-prevailing party to the dispute must pay the costs of the legal intervention and reasonable attorney's fees.

15 Limitation of Liability

Section 15 establishes that the broker and his or her associates will not be held responsible for the buyer's personal injuries or damage to the buyer's property.

16. Addenda

Section 16 includes any addenda or documents related to the Buyer Representation Agreement. This section also requires that an **Information About Brokerage Services** form be attached to the agreement. The Information About Brokerage Services is a promulgated form by the TREC that discloses the agency relationship between the agent and the principal. Texas real estate law requires an agent to give this form to sellers, buyers, landlords, and tenants.

17. Special Provisions

Section 17 provides a blank space where the broker may include any special provisions that are part of the Buyer Representation Agreement.

18. Additional Notices

The final section of the Buyer Representation Agreement, provides other important information about the agreement, relevant laws, and terms.

A. The broker's fees are not fixed, controlled, recommended, suggested, or maintained by the Association of REALTORS®, MLS, or any other listing service.

B. The broker must provide assistance without regard to race, color, religion, national origin, sex, disability, or familial status. Local ordinances may also provide additional protection.

C. Rather than utilizing a broker, the buyer should seek professional assistance regarding property inspection, surveying, environmental assessments, or compliance.

D. If the buyer purchases property, the buyer is advised to have an attorney examine an abstract covering the property or obtain title insurance.

E.   The buyer has the option of purchasing a **residential service contract**. This is a contract that offers home warranty services to maintain, repair or replace appliances, structural components, electrical, plumbing, heating, or air conditioning systems of residential property.

F.   The broker is unable to offer legal advice. An attorney should review the Buyer Representation Agreement prior to signing if it is unclear.

Summary

Buying real estate is one of the largest purchases a consumer may make in his or her lifetime. While some buyers believe that they can navigate through the complicated world of real estate on their own, most require the resources of an agent to simplify the process. A **buyer's agent** is a broker employed by the buyer to locate a certain kind of real property.

If a buyer is working exclusively with a broker or sales associate, the broker or sales associate must first present a written disclosure regarding the agency relationship before entering into an agreement. If the buyer is not working with the sales associate or broker exclusively, the selling agent (who may also be the listing agent) must provide a written disclosure regarding the agency relationship before the buyer makes an offer to purchase. The written disclosure that expresses this agency relationship is a Buyer Representation Agreement.

In a Texas real estate transaction, the **Residential Buyer/Tenant Representation Agreement** is the common contract form that creates an agency relationship between the buyer and the real estate broker. It is typically referred to as simply the **Buyer Representation Agreement**. The Texas Association of REALTORS® promulgates the form. The form entitles the real estate broker to a commission if the broker finds real property for the buyer or if the buyer finds the property on his or her own.

Each section of the Buyer Representation Agreement contains the pertinent details of the buyer's agency relationship with the real estate broker. Texas real estate licensees should be familiar with the form and be able to explain the content to clients.

Unit 6

Residential Purchase Agreement

Introduction

The residential purchase agreement is one of the most important contracts for real estate licensees to understand. The **purchase agreement**, or sales contract, sets the terms between the buyer and seller for the sale of real property. The contract contains information pertinent to the sale, including the identification of the parties, the purchase price, and the parties' rights and obligations. The most common type of residential sales contract in Texas is the **One To Four Family Residential Contract (Resale)**. This unit explains each section of this contract and how it affects the sale of real property.

Learning Objectives

After reading this unit, you should be able to:

- identify important elements in sales contracts.
- prepare real estate contracts.
- explain each section of the One To Four Family Residential Contract (Resale).
- complete a One To Four Family Residential Contract (Resale).

Sales Contracts in Real Estate

When a buyer purchases real property from a seller, the two parties are bound to a purchase agreement contract. In Texas, the purchase agreement is frequently referred to as the sales contract or the earnest money contract. The sales contract for real estate provides a comprehensive overview of the terms of the sale. The contract begins with basic information including the parties to the transaction, a property description, and the sales price. The contract then becomes more specific and additional information may be required. Important components of a valid sales contract include the offer and acceptance, earnest money, and equitable title.

The Offer and Acceptance

To create a valid sales contract, the buyer and seller must mutually agree to the terms of the sale. The **offer** and the acceptance of the terms serve as primary evidence for this requirement. A buyer suggests a purchase price and terms (an offer) to the agent who in turn presents that offer to the seller in the form of a sales contract. Once the seller reviews the offer and agrees to the terms, the seller signs the sales contract; this ultimately signifies **acceptance** of the offer. If the seller does not agree to the terms, he or she may adjust the terms of the sale, thus creating a **counteroffer**. The buyer may then accept, reject, or adjust the terms of the counteroffer and resubmit it to the seller. This process continues until one party accepts the offer or a final rejection is made by either party.

Earnest Money

Typically, a real estate sales transaction calls for the buyer to include a cash down payment. The real estate industry often refers to this payment as **earnest money**. The earnest money expresses a buyer's intent to honor the terms of the sales contract. The amount of earnest money may vary depending on the amount agreed on by the buyer and seller. Either way, the amount should be sufficient to convince the seller of the buyer's good faith in carrying out the terms of the sales contract. The buyer gives the earnest money to the agent who deposits it into a trust account or leaves it with an escrow agent once an offer is accepted.

Equitable Title

After both parties have signed the sales contract, the buyer receives equitable title to the property. **Equitable title** means the buyer holds an interest on property that is legally vested in the name of another person. The buyer, however, does not yet have legal title to the property. Legal title is acquired when both parties have met all terms of the sales contract and a title company or attorney issues a deed to the new owner.

One To Four Family Residential Contract (Resale)

A real estate broker or salesperson in Texas frequently encounters the One To Four Family Residential Contract (Resale). This sales contract, also known as TREC form 20-8, is promulgated by the Texas Real Estate Commission for residential property. In Texas, different versions of this contract exist based on the type of property for sale (for example, transactions that involve condominiums or commercial property). The residential contract is intended to be used for resale property and one to four family dwellings. It is not intended for use with new construction, larger residential or commercial units, or transactions that involve

condominiums. The special notice found just below the title of the contract indicates which type of form it is.

Caution: It is a violation of Section 16 of The Real Estate License Act for a licensee to use an out-of-date form. The date in the upper right-hand corner of the contract indicates when TREC promulgated the form. Be sure to check that date and use the most recent version from TREC.

Read the One To Four Family Residential Contract (Resale) and get to know it well. Understand the provisions of the form thoroughly and be able to explain them to your principal. When completing it, carefully enter accurate information. After completing the form, scan the contract and verify the accuracy of the information.

06-30-08

PROMULGATED BY THE TEXAS REAL ESTATE COMMISSION (TREC)

ONE TO FOUR FAMILY RESIDENTIAL CONTRACT (RESALE)

NOTICE: Not For Use For Condominium Transactions

1. PARTIES: The parties to this contract are _____(Seller) and _____(Buyer). Seller agrees to sell and convey to Buyer and Buyer agrees to buy from Seller the Property defined below.

2. PROPERTY:

A. LAND: Lot _____ Block_____, _____Addition, City of _____ , County of _____ Texas, known as _____(address/zip code), or as described on attached exhibit.

B. IMPROVEMENTS: The house, garage and all other fixtures and improvements attached to the above-described real property, including without limitation, the following **permanently installed and built-in items,** if any: all equipment and appliances, valances, screens, shutters, awnings, wall-to-wall carpeting, mirrors, ceiling fans, attic fans, mail boxes, television antennas and satellite dish system and equipment, heating and air-conditioning units, security and fire detection equipment, wiring, plumbing and lighting fixtures, chandeliers, water softener system, kitchen equipment, garage door openers, cleaning equipment, shrubbery, landscaping, outdoor cooking equipment, and all other property owned by Seller and attached to the above described real property.

C. ACCESSORIES: The following described related accessories, if any: window air conditioning units, stove, fireplace screens, curtains and rods, blinds, window shades, draperies and rods, controls for satellite dish system, controls for garage door openers, entry gate controls, door keys, mailbox keys, above ground pool, swimming pool equipment and maintenance accessories, and artificial fireplace logs.

D. EXCLUSIONS: The following improvements and accessories will be retained by Seller and must be removed prior to delivery of possession:_____ _____.

The land, improvements and accessories are collectively referred to as the "Property".

3. SALES PRICE:

A. Cash portion of Sales Price payable by Buyer at closing................. $_____

B. Sum of all financing described below (excluding any loan funding fee or mortgage insurance premium)... $_____

C. Sales Price (Sum of A and B).. $_____

4. FINANCING: The portion of Sales Price not payable in cash will be paid as follows: (Check applicable boxes below)

☐ A. THIRD PARTY FINANCING: One or more third party mortgage loans in the total amount of $_____ (excluding any loan funding fee or mortgage insurance premium).

(1) Property Approval: If the Property does not satisfy the lenders' underwriting requirements for the loan(s), this contract will terminate and the earnest money will be refunded to Buyer.

(2) Financing Approval: (Check one box only)

☐(a) This contract is subject to Buyer being approved for the financing described in the attached Third Party Financing Condition Addendum.

☐(b) This contract is not subject to Buyer being approved for financing and does not involve FHA or VA financing.

☐ B. ASSUMPTION: The assumption of the unpaid principal balance of one or more promissory notes described in the attached TREC Loan Assumption Addendum.

☐ C. SELLER FINANCING: A promissory note from Buyer to Seller of $_____, secured by vendor's and deed of trust liens, and containing the terms and conditions described in the attached TREC Seller Financing Addendum. If an owner policy of title insurance is furnished, Buyer shall furnish Seller with a mortgagee policy of title insurance.

5. EARNEST MONEY: Upon execution of this contract by all parties, Buyer shall deposit $_____ as earnest money with _____, as escrow agent, at _____ (address). Buyer shall deposit additional earnest money of $_____ with escrow agent within _____ days after the effective date of this contract. If Buyer fails to deposit the earnest money as required by this contract, Buyer will be in default.

6. TITLE POLICY AND SURVEY:

A. TITLE POLICY: Seller shall furnish to Buyer at ☐Seller's ☐Buyer's expense an owner policy of title insurance (Title Policy) issued by _____ (Title Company) in the amount of the Sales Price, dated at or after closing, insuring Buyer against loss under the provisions of the Title Policy, subject to the promulgated exclusions

Initialed for identification by Buyer_____ _____ and Seller _____ _____   TREC NO. 20-8

TEXAS LAW OF CONTRACTS

Contract Concerning _____ Page 2 of 8   06-30-08
(Address of Property)

(including existing building and zoning ordinances) and the following exceptions:
(1) Restrictive covenants common to the platted subdivision in which the Property is located.
(2) The standard printed exception for standby fees, taxes and assessments.
(3) Liens created as part of the financing described in Paragraph 4.
(4) Utility easements created by the dedication deed or plat of the subdivision in which the Property is located.
(5) Reservations or exceptions otherwise permitted by this contract or as may be approved by Buyer in writing.
(6) The standard printed exception as to marital rights.
(7) The standard printed exception as to waters, tidelands, beaches, streams, and related matters.
(8) The standard printed exception as to discrepancies, conflicts, shortages in area or boundary lines, encroachments or protrusions, or overlapping improvements. Buyer, at Buyer's expense, may have the exception amended to read, "shortages in area".

B. COMMITMENT: Within 20 days after the Title Company receives a copy of this contract, Seller shall furnish to Buyer a commitment for title insurance (Commitment) and, at Buyer's expense, legible copies of restrictive covenants and documents evidencing exceptions in the Commitment (Exception Documents) other than the standard printed exceptions. Seller authorizes the Title Company to deliver the Commitment and Exception Documents to Buyer at Buyer's address shown in Paragraph 21. If the Commitment and Exception Documents are not delivered to Buyer within the specified time, the time for delivery will be automatically extended up to 15 days or the Closing Date, whichever is earlier.

C. SURVEY: The survey must be made by a registered professional land surveyor acceptable to the Title Company and Buyer's lender(s). (Check one box only)
   ☐ (1) Within _____ days after the effective date of this contract, Seller shall furnish to Buyer and Title Company Seller's existing survey of the Property and a Residential Real Property Affidavit promulgated by the Texas Department of Insurance (Affidavit). If the existing survey or Affidavit is not acceptable to Title Company or Buyer's lender(s), Buyer shall obtain a new survey at ☐ Seller's ☐ Buyer's expense no later than 3 days prior to Closing Date. **If Seller fails to furnish the existing survey or Affidavit within the time prescribed, Buyer shall obtain a new survey at Seller's expense no later than 3 days prior to Closing Date.**
   ☐ (2) Within _____ days after the effective date of this contract, Buyer shall obtain a new survey at Buyer's expense. Buyer is deemed to receive the survey on the date of actual receipt or the date specified in this paragraph, whichever is earlier.
   ☐ (3) Within _____ days after the effective date of this contract, Seller, at Seller's expense shall furnish a new survey to Buyer.

D. OBJECTIONS: Buyer may object in writing to defects, exceptions, or encumbrances to title: disclosed on the survey other than items 6A(1) through (7) above; disclosed in the Commitment other than items 6A(1) through (8) above; or which prohibit the following use or activity: _____
_____.
Buyer must object the earlier of (i) the Closing Date or (ii) _____ days after Buyer receives the Commitment, Exception Documents, and the survey. Buyer's failure to object within the time allowed will constitute a waiver of Buyer's right to object; except that the requirements in Schedule C of the Commitment are not waived. Provided Seller is not obligated to incur any expense, Seller shall cure the timely objections of Buyer or any third party lender within 15 days after Seller receives the objections and the Closing Date will be extended as necessary. If objections are not cured within such 15 day period, this contract will terminate and the earnest money will be refunded to Buyer unless Buyer waives the objections.

E. TITLE NOTICES:
   (1) ABSTRACT OR TITLE POLICY: Broker advises Buyer to have an abstract of title covering the Property examined by an attorney of Buyer's selection, or Buyer should be furnished with or obtain a Title Policy. If a Title Policy is furnished, the Commitment should be promptly reviewed by an attorney of Buyer's choice due to the time limitations on Buyer's right to object.
   (2) PROPERTY OWNERS' ASSOCIATION MANDATORY MEMBERSHIP: The Property ☐ is ☐ is not subject to mandatory membership in a property owners' association. If the Property is subject to mandatory membership in a property owners' association, Seller notifies Buyer under §5.012, Texas Property Code, that, as a purchaser of property in the residential community identified in Paragraph 2A in which the Property is located, you are obligated to be a member of the property owners' association. Restrictive covenants governing the use and occupancy of the Property and a dedicatory instrument governing the establishment, maintenance, and operation of this residential community have been or will be recorded in the Real Property Records of the county in which the Property is located. Copies of the restrictive covenants and dedicatory instrument may be obtained from the county clerk. You are obligated to pay assessments to the property owners' association. The amount of the assessments is subject to change. Your failure to pay the

Initialed for identification by Buyer_____ _____ and Seller _____ _____   TREC NO. 20-8

Unit 6: Residential Purchase Agreement

assessments could result in a lien on and the foreclosure of the Property. **If Buyer is concerned about these matters, the TREC promulgated Addendum for Property Subject to Mandatory Membership in a Property Owners' Association should be used.**

(3) STATUTORY TAX DISTRICTS: If the Property is situated in a utility or other statutorily created district providing water, sewer, drainage, or flood control facilities and services, Chapter 49, Texas Water Code, requires Seller to deliver and Buyer to sign the statutory notice relating to the tax rate, bonded indebtedness, or standby fee of the district prior to final execution of this contract.

(4) TIDE WATERS: If the Property abuts the tidally influenced waters of the state, §33.135, Texas Natural Resources Code, requires a notice regarding coastal area property to be included in the contract. An addendum containing the notice promulgated by TREC or required by the parties must be used.

(5) ANNEXATION: If the Property is located outside the limits of a municipality, Seller notifies Buyer under §5.011, Texas Property Code, that the Property may now or later be included in the extraterritorial jurisdiction of a municipality and may now or later be subject to annexation by the municipality. Each municipality maintains a map that depicts its boundaries and extraterritorial jurisdiction. To determine if the Property is located within a municipality's extraterritorial jurisdiction or is likely to be located within a municipality's extraterritorial jurisdiction, contact all municipalities located in the general proximity of the Property for further information.

(6) PROPERTY LOCATED IN A CERTIFICATED SERVICE AREA OF A UTILITY SERVICE PROVIDER: Notice required by §13.257, Water Code: The real property, described in Paragraph 2, that you are about to purchase may be located in a certificated water or sewer service area, which is authorized by law to provide water or sewer service to the properties in the certificated area. If your property is located in a certificated area there may be special costs or charges that you will be required to pay before you can receive water or sewer service. There may be a period required to construct lines or other facilities necessary to provide water or sewer service to your property. You are advised to determine if the property is in a certificated area and contact the utility service provider to determine the cost that you will be required to pay and the period, if any, that is required to provide water or sewer service to your property. The undersigned Buyer hereby acknowledges receipt of the foregoing notice at or before the execution of a binding contract for the purchase of the real property described in Paragraph 2 or at closing of purchase of the real property.

(7) PUBLIC IMPROVEMENT DISTRICTS: If the Property is in a public improvement district, §5.014, Property Code, requires Seller to notify Buyer as follows: As a purchaser of this parcel of real property you are obligated to pay an assessment to a municipality or county for an improvement project undertaken by a public improvement district under Chapter 372, Local Government Code. The assessment may be due annually or in periodic installments. More information concerning the amount of the assessment and the due dates of that assessment may be obtained from the municipality or county levying the assessment. The amount of the assessments is subject to change. Your failure to pay the assessments could result in a lien on and the foreclosure of your property.

7. **PROPERTY CONDITION:**
    A. ACCESS, INSPECTIONS AND UTILITIES: Seller shall permit Buyer and Buyer's agents access to the Property at reasonable times. Buyer may have the Property inspected by inspectors selected by Buyer and licensed by TREC or otherwise permitted by law to make inspections. Seller at Seller's expense shall turn on existing utilities for inspections.
    B. SELLER'S DISCLOSURE NOTICE PURSUANT TO §5.008, TEXAS PROPERTY CODE (Notice): (Check one box only)
      ☐ (1) Buyer has received the Notice.
      ☐ (2) Buyer has not received the Notice. Within _____ days after the effective date of this contract, Seller shall deliver the Notice to Buyer. If Buyer does not receive the Notice, Buyer may terminate this contract at any time prior to the closing and the earnest money will be refunded to Buyer. If Seller delivers the Notice, Buyer may terminate this contract for any reason within 7 days after Buyer receives the Notice or prior to the closing, whichever first occurs, and the earnest money will be refunded to Buyer.
      ☐ (3) The Seller is not required to furnish the notice under the Texas Property Code.
    C. SELLER'S DISCLOSURE OF LEAD-BASED PAINT AND LEAD-BASED PAINT HAZARDS is required by Federal law for a residential dwelling constructed prior to 1978.
    D. ACCEPTANCE OF PROPERTY CONDITION: (Check one box only)
      ☐ (1) Buyer accepts the Property in its present condition.
      ☐ (2) Buyer accepts the Property in its present condition provided Seller, at Seller's expense, shall complete the following specific repairs and treatments: _____.
    E. LENDER REQUIRED REPAIRS AND TREATMENTS: Unless otherwise agreed in writing, neither party is obligated to pay for lender required repairs, which includes treatment

Initialed for identification by Buyer_____ _____ and Seller _____ _____   TREC NO. 20-8

TEXAS LAW OF CONTRACTS

for wood destroying insects. If the parties do not agree to pay for the lender required repairs or treatments, this contract will terminate and the earnest money will be refunded to Buyer.   If the cost of lender required repairs and treatments exceeds 5% of the Sales Price, Buyer may terminate this contract and the earnest money will be refunded to Buyer.

F. COMPLETION OF REPAIRS AND TREATMENTS: Unless otherwise agreed in writing, Seller shall complete all agreed repairs and treatments prior to the Closing Date. All required permits must be obtained, and repairs and treatments must be performed by persons who are licensed or otherwise authorized by law to provide such repairs or treatments. At Buyer's election, any transferable warranties received by Seller with respect to the repairs and treatments will be transferred to Buyer at Buyer's expense. If Seller fails to complete any agreed repairs and treatments prior to the Closing Date, Buyer may do so and receive reimbursement from Seller at closing. The Closing Date will be extended up to 15 days, if necessary, to complete repairs and treatments.

G. ENVIRONMENTAL MATTERS: Buyer is advised that the presence of wetlands, toxic substances, including asbestos and wastes or other environmental hazards, or the presence of a threatened or endangered species or its habitat may affect Buyer's intended use of the Property. If Buyer is concerned about these matters, an addendum promulgated by TREC or required by the parties should be used.

H. RESIDENTIAL SERVICE CONTRACTS: Buyer may purchase a residential service contract from a residential service company licensed by TREC. If Buyer purchases a residential service contract, Seller shall reimburse Buyer at closing for the cost of the residential service contract in an amount not exceeding $_____.   Buyer should review any residential service contract for the scope of coverage, exclusions and limitations. **The purchase of a residential service contract is optional. Similar coverage may be purchased from various companies authorized to do business in Texas.**

8. **BROKERS' FEES:** All obligations of the parties for payment of brokers' fees are contained in separate written agreements.

9. **CLOSING:**

A. The closing of the sale will be on or before _____, 20____, or within 7 days after objections made under Paragraph 6D have been cured or waived, whichever date is later (Closing Date). If either party fails to close the sale by the Closing Date, the non-defaulting party may exercise the remedies contained in Paragraph 15.

B. At closing:
(1) Seller shall execute and deliver a general warranty deed conveying title to the Property to Buyer and showing no additional exceptions to those permitted in Paragraph 6 and furnish tax statements or certificates showing no delinquent taxes on the Property.
(2) Buyer shall pay the Sales Price in good funds acceptable to the escrow agent.
(3) Seller and Buyer shall execute and deliver any notices, statements, certificates, affidavits, releases, loan documents and other documents required of them by this contract, the Commitment or law necessary for the closing of the sale and the issuance of the Title Policy.
(4) There will be no liens, assessments, or security interests against the Property which will not be satisfied out of the sales proceeds unless securing the payment of any loans assumed by Buyer and assumed loans will not be in default.

10. **POSSESSION:** Seller shall deliver to Buyer possession of the Property in its present or required condition, ordinary wear and tear excepted: ☐ upon closing and funding ☐ according to a temporary residential lease form promulgated by TREC or other written lease required by the parties. Any possession by Buyer prior to closing or by Seller after closing which is not authorized by a written lease will establish a tenancy at sufferance relationship between the parties. **Consult your insurance agent prior to change of ownership and possession because insurance coverage may be limited or terminated. The absence of a written lease or appropriate insurance coverage may expose the parties to economic loss.**

11. **SPECIAL PROVISIONS:** (Insert only factual statements and business details applicable to the sale. TREC rules prohibit licensees from adding factual statements or business details for which a contract addendum, lease or other form has been promulgated by TREC for mandatory use.)

Initialed for identification by Buyer_____ _____ and Seller _____ _____   TREC NO. 20-8

Contract Concerning _____ Page 5 of 8   06-30-08
(Address of Property)

12. SETTLEMENT AND OTHER EXPENSES:
    A. The following expenses must be paid at or prior to closing:
      (1) Expenses payable by Seller (Seller's Expenses):
        (a) Releases of existing liens, including prepayment penalties and recording fees; release of Seller's loan liability; tax statements or certificates; preparation of deed; one-half of escrow fee; and other expenses payable by Seller under this contract.
        (b) Seller shall also pay an amount not to exceed $ _____ to be applied in the following order: Buyer's Expenses which Buyer is prohibited from paying by FHA, VA, Texas Veterans Land Board or other governmental loan programs, and then to other Buyer's Expenses as allowed by the lender.
      (2) Expenses payable by Buyer (Buyer's Expenses):
        (a) Loan origination, discount, buy-down, and commitment fees (Loan Fees).
        (b) Appraisal fees; loan application fees; credit reports; preparation of loan documents; interest on the notes from date of disbursement to one month prior to dates of first monthly payments; recording fees; copies of easements and restrictions; mortgagee title policy with endorsements required by lender; loan-related inspection fees; photos; amortization schedules; one-half of escrow fee; all prepaid items, including required premiums for flood and hazard insurance, reserve deposits for insurance, ad valorem taxes and special governmental assessments; final compliance inspection; courier fee; repair inspection; underwriting fee; wire transfer fee; expenses incident to any loan; and other expenses payable by Buyer under this contract.
    B. Buyer shall pay Private Mortgage Insurance Premium (PMI), VA Loan Funding Fee, or FHA Mortgage Insurance Premium (MIP) as required by the lender.
    C. If any expense exceeds an amount expressly stated in this contract for such expense to be paid by a party, that party may terminate this contract unless the other party agrees to pay such excess. Buyer may not pay charges and fees expressly prohibited by FHA, VA, Texas Veterans Land Board or other governmental loan program regulations.

13. PRORATIONS: Taxes for the current year, interest, maintenance fees, assessments, dues and rents will be prorated through the Closing Date. The tax proration may be calculated taking into consideration any change in exemptions that will affect the current year's taxes. If taxes for the current year vary from the amount prorated at closing, the parties shall adjust the prorations when tax statements for the current year are available. If taxes are not paid at or prior to closing, Buyer shall pay taxes for the current year.

14. CASUALTY LOSS: If any part of the Property is damaged or destroyed by fire or other casualty after the effective date of this contract, Seller shall restore the Property to its previous condition as soon as reasonably possible, but in any event by the Closing Date. If Seller fails to do so due to factors beyond Seller's control, Buyer may (a) terminate this contract and the earnest money will be refunded to Buyer (b) extend the time for performance up to 15 days and the Closing Date will be extended as necessary or (c) accept the Property in its damaged condition with an assignment of insurance proceeds and receive credit from Seller at closing in the amount of the deductible under the insurance policy. Seller's obligations under this paragraph are independent of any other obligations of Seller under this contract.

15. DEFAULT: If Buyer fails to comply with this contract, Buyer will be in default, and Seller may (a) enforce specific performance, seek such other relief as may be provided by law, or both, or (b) terminate this contract and receive the earnest money as liquidated damages, thereby releasing both parties from this contract. If, due to factors beyond Seller's control, Seller fails within the time allowed to make any non-casualty repairs or deliver the Commitment, or survey, if required of Seller, Buyer may (a) extend the time for performance up to 15 days and the Closing Date will be extended as necessary or (b) terminate this contract as the sole remedy and receive the earnest money. If Seller fails to comply with this contract for any other reason, Seller will be in default and Buyer may (a) enforce specific performance, seek such other relief as may be provided by law, or both, or (b) terminate this contract and receive the earnest money, thereby releasing both parties from this contract.

16. MEDIATION: It is the policy of the State of Texas to encourage resolution of disputes through alternative dispute resolution procedures such as mediation. Any dispute between Seller and Buyer related to this contract which is not resolved through informal discussion ❑will ❑will not be submitted to a mutually acceptable mediation service or provider. The parties to the mediation shall bear the mediation costs equally. This paragraph does not preclude a party from seeking equitable relief from a court of competent jurisdiction.

17. ATTORNEY'S FEES: A Buyer, Seller, Listing Broker, Other Broker, or escrow agent who prevails in any legal proceeding related to this contract is entitled to recover reasonable attorney's fees and all costs of such proceeding.

Initialed for identification by Buyer_____ _____ and Seller _____ _____   TREC NO. 20-8

Contract Concerning _____ Page 6 of 8   06-30-08
(Address of Property)

18. ESCROW:
A. ESCROW: The escrow agent is not (i) a party to this contract and does not have liability for the performance or nonperformance of any party to this contract, (ii) liable for interest on the earnest money and (iii) liable for the loss of any earnest money caused by the failure of any financial institution in which the earnest money has been deposited unless the financial institution is acting as escrow agent.
B. EXPENSES: At closing, the earnest money must be applied first to any cash down payment, then to Buyer's Expenses and any excess refunded to Buyer. If no closing occurs, escrow agent may require payment of unpaid expenses incurred on behalf of the parties and a written release of liability of escrow agent from all parties.
C. DEMAND: Upon termination of this contract, either party or the escrow agent may send a release of earnest money to each party and the parties shall execute counterparts of the release and deliver same to the escrow agent. If either party fails to execute the release, either party may make a written demand to the escrow agent for the earnest money. If only one party makes written demand for the earnest money, escrow agent shall promptly provide a copy of the demand to the other party. If escrow agent does not receive written objection to the demand from the other party within 15 days, escrow agent may disburse the earnest money to the party making demand reduced by the amount of unpaid expenses incurred on behalf of the party receiving the earnest money and escrow agent may pay the same to the creditors. If escrow agent complies with the provisions of this paragraph, each party hereby releases escrow agent from all adverse claims related to the disbursal of the earnest money.
D. DAMAGES: Any party who wrongfully fails or refuses to sign a release acceptable to the escrow agent within 7 days of receipt of the request will be liable to the other party for liquidated damages in an amount equal to the sum of: (i) three times the amount of the earnest money; (ii) the earnest money; (iii) reasonable attorney's fees; and (iv) all costs of suit.
E. NOTICES: Escrow agent's notices will be effective when sent in compliance with Paragraph 21. Notice of objection to the demand will be deemed effective upon receipt by escrow agent.

19. REPRESENTATIONS: All covenants, representations and warranties in this contract survive closing. If any representation of Seller in this contract is untrue on the Closing Date, Seller will be in default. Unless expressly prohibited by written agreement, Seller may continue to show the Property and receive, negotiate and accept back up offers.

20. FEDERAL TAX REQUIREMENTS: If Seller is a "foreign person," as defined by applicable law, or if Seller fails to deliver an affidavit to Buyer that Seller is not a "foreign person," then Buyer shall withhold from the sales proceeds an amount sufficient to comply with applicable tax law and deliver the same to the Internal Revenue Service together with appropriate tax forms. Internal Revenue Service regulations require filing written reports if currency in excess of specified amounts is received in the transaction.

21. NOTICES: All notices from one party to the other must be in writing and are effective when mailed to, hand-delivered at, or transmitted by facsimile or electronic transmission as follows:

To Buyer	**To Seller**
at: _____	at: _____
_____	_____
_____	_____
_____	_____
Telephone: ( ) _____	Telephone: ( ) _____
Facsimile: ( ) _____	Facsimile: ( ) _____
E-mail: _____	E-mail: _____

Initialed for identification by Buyer_____ _____ and Seller _____ _____   TREC NO. 20-8

Contract Concerning _____ Page 7 of 8   06-30-08
(Address of Property)

22. AGREEMENT OF PARTIES: This contract contains the entire agreement of the parties and cannot be changed except by their written agreement. Addenda which are a part of this contract are (Check all applicable boxes):

❏ Third Party Financing Condition Addendum

❏ Seller Financing Addendum

❏ Addendum for Property Subject to Mandatory Membership in a Property Owners' Association

❏ Buyer's Temporary Residential Lease

❏ Seller's Temporary Residential Lease

❏ Addendum for Sale of Other Property by Buyer

❏ Addendum Containing Required Notices Under §5.016, §420.001 and §420.002, Texas Property Code

❏ Addendum for "Back-Up" Contract

❏ Addendum for Coastal Area Property

❏ Environmental Assessment, Threatened or Endangered Species and Wetlands Addendum

❏ Addendum for Property Located Seaward of the Gulf Intracoastal Waterway

❏ Addendum for Seller's Disclosure of Information on Lead-based Paint and Lead-based Paint Hazards as Required by Federal Law

❏ Other (list): _____

_____

23. TERMINATION OPTION: For nominal consideration, the receipt of which is hereby acknowledged by Seller, and Buyer's agreement to pay Seller $_____ (Option Fee) within 2 days after the effective date of this contract, Seller grants Buyer the unrestricted right to terminate this contract by giving notice of termination to Seller within _____ days after the effective date of this contract. If no dollar amount is stated as the Option Fee or if Buyer fails to pay the Option Fee to Seller within the time prescribed, this paragraph will not be a part of this contract and Buyer shall not have the unrestricted right to terminate this contract. If Buyer gives notice of termination within the time prescribed, the Option Fee will not be refunded; however, any earnest money will be refunded to Buyer. The Option Fee ❏will ❏will not be credited to the Sales Price at closing. **Time is of the essence for this paragraph and strict compliance with the time for performance is required.**

24. CONSULT AN ATTORNEY: Real estate licensees cannot give legal advice. READ THIS CONTRACT CAREFULLY. If you do not understand the effect of this contract, consult an attorney BEFORE signing.

Buyer's
Attorney is: _____

Seller's
Attorney is: _____

_____

_____

Telephone: ( )_____

Telephone: ( )_____

Facsimile: ( )_____

Facsimile: ( )_____

E-mail: _____

E-mail: _____

> **EXECUTED the _____ day of _____, 20_____ (EFFECTIVE DATE).**
> **(BROKER: FILL IN THE DATE OF FINAL ACCEPTANCE.)**

_____
Buyer

_____
Seller

_____
Buyer

_____
Seller

TREC NO. 20-8

TEXAS LAW OF CONTRACTS

Contract Concerning _____ Page 8 of 8   06-30-08
(Address of Property)

BROKER INFORMATION AND RATIFICATION OF FEE

Listing Broker has agreed to pay Other Broker _____ of   the total sales price when Listing Broker's fee is received. Escrow Agent is authorized and directed to pay Other Broker from Listing Broker's fee at closing.

Other Broker License No.	Listing Broker License No.
represents ☐ Buyer only as Buyer's agent	represents ☐ Seller and Buyer as an intermediary
☐ Seller as Listing Broker's subagent	☐ Seller only as Seller's agent
Associate Telephone	Listing Associate Telephone
Broker's Address	Listing Associate's Office Address Facsimile
City State Zip	City State Zip
Facsimile	Email Address
Email Address	Selling Associate Telephone
	Selling Associate's Office Address Facsimile
	City State Zip
	Email Address

OPTION FEE RECEIPT

Receipt of $_____ (Option Fee) in the form of _____ is acknowledged.

_____   _____
Seller or Listing Broker   Date

CONTRACT AND EARNEST MONEY RECEIPT

Receipt of ☐Contract and ☐$_____ Earnest Money in the form of _____
is acknowledged.
Escrow Agent: _____   Date: _____

By: _____   _____
                                                                                    Email Address

_____   Telephone (_____) _____
Address

_____   Facsimile: (_____) _____
City   State   Zip

TREC NO. 20-8

Case Study

The information in this case study is used to complete the One To Four Family Residential Contract (Resale).

The Sellers

Fred and Jan Spring own a single-family detached home in the Hillside Ranch subdivision located at 1652 Hill Street, Big City, Apple County, Texas 70000. The property's legal description is Lot 2 of Block 30 of Hillside Ranch, as shown on page 875 of book 465, records of Apple County.

Fred and Jan's telephone number is (806) 000-0000 and their fax machine is (806) 000-0001. Their e-mail address is thesprings@bigcity.xyz.

Because their home is part of a planned community with common areas, the Spring's currently pay $209 monthly for homeowners' association dues. The annual property taxes are $1,500 and are paid current by the seller. The current loan balance on the property is $155,485.

Due to a change in Fred Spring's career, he and his family must sell their home and move to another state. Based on the amount that other homes have sold for in their neighborhood, Fred and Jan believe their home should sell for about $235,000.

Seller's Broker

Pat Green is a sales associate working for Tom Baker who is the broker-owner of Sunshine Real Estate. Sunshine Real Estate is located at 567 8th Street, Freedom, TX 70001. The phone number is (806) 765-4321, the fax is (806)123-4568, and the e-mail is pgreen@sunshinere.xyz. Pat wants to get a listing on the Spring's home. Pat is familiar with the homes in the Hillside Ranch area and has had many recent sales there.

Hillside Ranch has 150 single-family homes ranging in value from $150,000 to $250,000, with an average sales price of $225,000. After researching recent sales and current market activity, Pat determined that the Spring's home should list for $210,000 to $225,000. Since the Springs need to move as soon as possible, they decide to give the broker, Tom Baker, a 3-month listing on their home for $215,000 with a 6% commission. The buyer's broker will receive 2.5% of the commission. The Springs will not pay an amount more than $1,000 to cover buyer expenses at closing.

The Buyers

Sam and Cindy Winter, a newly married couple who currently live at 123 Triangle Square, Geometry, Texas 76543 would like to buy the Spring's home, located at 1652 Hill Street, Big City, Apple County, Texas, 70000. The buyers' telephone number is (214) 000-0000 and their fax machine is (214) 000-0001. Sam and Cindy's e-mail address is thewinters@geometry.xyz.

On April 15, 20xx, the Winters signed an offer to purchase and an earnest money deposit for the home. The Winters offered $215,000. The buyers would like escrow to close in forty-five (45) days, on or before June 30, 20xx. The buyers gave a check for $5,000 as an earnest money deposit. If the offer is accepted, they will increase the deposit to a total of $43,000 when escrow is opened. Prior to close, the balance of the deposit, $38,000, will be deposited into escrow. The Winters plan to get a conventional 80%, fully amortized, 30-year loan, with a fixed interest rate not to exceed 6% and 2 points.

Based on this information, the buyers' salesperson, Linda Rose, calculated that their estimated monthly payment will be about $1,452 (principal and interest - $1,018, taxes - $125, insurance - $100, and association dues - $209).

Buyers' Broker

The Winters have buyer's representation with salesperson Linda Rose who works for Lisa Summers, broker of First Real Estate. The brokerage office is located at 123 4th Street, Walker, Texas, 70002. The phone number is (214) 111-1111, the fax is (214) 111-1112, and e-mail is lrose@firstrealestate.xyz.

When escrow closes, the commission will be paid to Lisa Summers, the broker. Lisa, in turn, will pay Linda Rose a commission based on their agreed-upon commission split (2.5% of the purchase price). Since the buyers will be obtaining a loan, the Third Party Financing Condition Addendum will accompany the sales contract. Also, an Addendum For Property Subject to Mandatory Membership in an Owners' Association is necessary since the property is in a planned community with common areas.

Other Stipulations

The sellers are responsible for furnishing the buyer with a title policy at the seller's expense. The escrow agent for this transaction is Any Title Company located at 321 Closing Avenue, Title, Texas 76543. The phone number is (000) 000-0000 and the fax is (000) 000-0001. The e-mail address for the escrow agent is escrow@anytitle.xyz.

The buyers are responsible for obtaining a survey on the property within seven days from the date of the contract. Once the buyer receives the title commitment, exception documents, and survey, they have no more than ten days to object to anything that affects title to the property.

At this time, the buyers received a copy of the Seller's Disclosure of Property Condition form. They have decided to accept the property at its present condition if the sellers replace three window screens. Possession of the property will take place at closing. The buyers also decide to pay $150 for a 14-day termination option, which will not apply to the sales price at closing.

Completing the Form

A real estate licensee must comprehend each section in the sales contract and be knowledgeable enough to explain each one to the principal. While completing the form, the licensee must maintain a high level of accuracy and provide all necessary information.

Based on the information provided in the case study above, each section below includes the information needed to complete the form.

1. Parties

The first section of the contract introduces the parties in the transaction - the buyer and the seller. It also indicates that the seller is willing to convey his or her property and the buyer is willing to purchase the property.

Accuracy is important when filling out this section. Be sure to verify the name of the seller by checking the owner's title policy or examining the name that appears on the deed used to convey the title. Use and spell legal names correctly. If the party is a married couple, state this specifically in this section.

"Fred Spring and wife, Jan Spring (Seller)" or "Fred and Jan Spring, Husband and Wife (Seller)"

"Sam Winter and wife, Cindy Winter (Buyer)" or "Sam and Cindy Winter, Husband and Wife (Buyer)"

2. Property

One of the valid requirements of a real estate contract is a legal description. The Texas Statute of Frauds also requires a legal description for any agreement that affects title to real property. This section defines the legal description of the property for sale. The description of the property must be definitive and accurate. It must be stated clearly, so that one can easily identify the property given the legal description alone.

Included in this section is a blank space for the lot number, block number, subdivision name, city, and postal address. Always verify the accuracy of the property description and ensure that the address correctly corresponds with the property for sale. Entering the wrong address or an incorrect property description could hold the licensee responsible for negligence. If you are unsure of the correct address of the property, validate it with the county clerk.

Section 2 also states the types of improvements and accessories included in the sale of the property. Any fixtures or exclusions that will not transfer with the sale should be noted here.

> **Lot 2, Block 30, Hillside Ranch Subdivision, City of Big City, County of Apple, Texas, known as 1652 Hill Street 70000**

3. Sales Price

Section 3 specifies the **sales price** of the property. Spaces are provided for the amount of cash the buyer will apply toward the purchase and the amount of financing the buyer will obtain. The sum of these two amounts constitutes the sales price.

If the buyer provides a cash down payment of $20,000 and seeks a loan from a savings bank for $100,000, then the sales price is $120,000 ($20,000 + $100,000).

   A. $43,000
   B. $172,000
   C. $215,000

4. Financing

Section 4 provides information regarding financing options the buyer may choose to purchase the property. Because most transactions do not involve a full cash purchase, three options for financing are presented. These options are third party financing, assumption, and seller financing. This section does not limit the buyer to only one option; the buyer may choose a combination of any of the three. Each type of financing requires a separate addendum attached to the sales contract. The use and purpose of addenda in the contract is discussed later in this unit.

A. Third Party Financing

Third party financing refers to the securing of funds from an outside source to finance a purchase. In real property, third party financing is typically related to a buyer obtaining a loan from a mortgage company.

Two boxes appear in Section 4A and address the buyer as subject to a lender's approval for third party financing. If the buyer is subject to approval from a lender, then a TREC Third Party Financing Condition Addendum form is attached to the sales contract. This form describes the nature of the financing the buyer obtains to purchase real property.

☑ **A. THIRD PARTY FINANCING: . . . in the total amount of $172,000.**

B. Assumption

When financing through assumption, the buyer seeks to assume the seller's existing loan. This type of financing requires a TREC Loan Assumption Addendum form, which provides the essential details of the loan assumption arrangement.

C. Seller Financing

Another option for financing allows the seller to assist the purchase of the property by offering the buyer a loan payable with interest. This option usually involves a promise to pay or a promissory note given by the buyer to the seller. The amount of the promissory note is included in this section. Seller financing requires TREC Seller Financing Addendum.

5. Earnest Money

Section 5 specifically addresses the handling of earnest money. As discussed earlier in this unit, earnest money demonstrates good faith on the buyer's behalf in carrying out the provisions of the sales contract. In addition, the earnest money deposit provides liquidated damages in the event that the buyer defaults on the contract. The amount of earnest money is usually between 3 to 5% of the sales price. Ultimately, the buyer and seller agree on the final amount of earnest money.

Extra blanks in this section are available if the buyer is unable to give the full deposit during the signing of the agreement. The buyer may opt to deposit more funds later, at a date specified in this section. If the buyer is then unable to deposit the funds at the specified date, he or she will be in default of the sales contract.

You must comply with TREC Rule 535.15, which states that earnest money must be deposited with an escrow holder by the second business day after signing the sales contract. Escrow is discussed later in this unit.

6. Title Policy and Survey

Section addresses title insurance. **Title insurance** is a contract that protects a property owner against loss if the title to the property is defective. Before issuing title insurance, a title insurance company performs a title check of a property's chain of ownership records. This is done to be sure that there is no question about who owns the property when ownership is transferred.

Section 6 also contains information regarding who pays for the title insurance, the name of the title insurance company, and any known exceptions to a clear title, such as a utility easement, that the buyer would accept as part of the title.

A. Title Policy

Most real estate transactions closed in Texas typically involve the issuance of a title policy to the purchaser of the property. It is also customary for the seller to cover the costs for obtaining the title insurance policy. However, these costs may be negotiated between the buyer and the seller.

> ☑ **TITLE POLICY:** Seller shall furnish to buyer at ☑ Seller's Expense an owner policy of title insurance (Title Policy) issued by Any Title Company

B. Commitment

This portion of Section 6 states that the seller must furnish the buyer with a commitment for title insurance. This must be done within 20 days of the title company receiving a copy of the sales contract.

C. Survey

A **survey** is a measurement of real property by a licensed surveyor in order to identify any easements or encroachments. This section determines when the survey of the property will be completed and which party is responsible for the costs.

> ☑ **(2) Within 7 days after the effective date of this contract,** . . .

D. Objections

After receiving a copy of the title check and the survey, the buyer has the option to object to the results if anything unsatisfactory is found in the reports. This can include things, such as encumbrances affecting good title to the property or any encroachments that may exist. If the buyer objects, the seller has 15 days to fix the defects, or the contract terminates.

D: Objections: Within 10 days after . . .

E. Title Notices

This portion of Section 6 addresses statutory notices a buyer should receive under specific circumstances. These notices will also require addenda.

1. Notice that the buyer should have an abstract of title covering the property examined by an attorney, or the buyer should be furnished with or obtain a title policy. An **abstract of title** is a summary of recorded documents that contain information that may affect title to real property.

2. Notice concerning restrictions and covenants if the property is under the control of a homeowners' association.

. . . The property ☑ is subject to mandatory membership in an owners' association.

3. Notice indicating whether the property is situated in a special utility tax district.

4. Notice concerning the location of a property near tide waters.

5. Notice showing that the property rests outside a municipality and may be subject to annexation by that municipality.

6. Notice showing that the property lies within a certificated service area of a utility service provider. This is a specific area that provides water and sewer services to property owners.

7. Notice showing that the property rests in a public improvement district. Properties located in a public improvement district require owners to pay special assessments that fund projects.

7. Property Condition

It is the duty of the licensee to avoid creating false expectations for the buyer regarding the condition of the property. When asked specific questions about the condition of the property, it is wise to avoid giving an opinion; instead, advise the buyer to have the property inspected.

Section 7 of the sales contract addresses the buyer's right to have a licensed home inspector examine the condition of the property. A related section, Section 23, gives the buyer the option to purchase the right to terminate the sales contract in the event that he or she receives information that would adversely affect the decision to purchase the property.

Professionals who may be helpful when evaluating properties
- TREC licensed real estate inspectors
- Structural engineers
- Electricians
- Plumbers
- Pest control specialists
- Heating and air conditioning contractors
- Lead inspectors
- Governmental agencies
- Environmental specialists

This section reserves the buyer's right to access the property during reasonable hours in order to perform the necessary inspections. This section instructs the seller to have the utilities switched on if required by the inspectors.

Section 5.008 of the Texas Property Code requires sellers of previously occupied residential dwelling units to provide buyers with a seller's disclosure notice with content and information required by statute. If the seller fails to provide a disclosure notice regarding the condition of the property before signing the sales agreement, the contract becomes voidable. If the seller provides the disclosure notice after signing the sales contract, the buyer has up to seven days to terminate the contract without the risk of losing earnest money.

Eleven exceptions to Section 5.008 of the Texas Property Code as stated in subsection (e)

This section does not apply to a transfer:

1. pursuant to a court order or foreclosure sale.
2. by a trustee in bankruptcy.
3. to a mortgagee by a mortgagor or successor in interest, or to a beneficiary of a deed of trust or successor in interest.
4. by a mortgagee or a beneficiary under a deed of trust who has acquired the real property at a sale conducted pursuant to a power of sale under a deed of trust or a sale pursuant to a court ordered foreclosure or has acquired the real property by a deed in lieu of foreclosure.
5. by a fiduciary in the course of the administration of a decedent's estate, guardianship, conservatorship, or trust.
6. from one co-owner to one or more additional co-owners.
7. made to a spouse or to a person or persons in the lineal line of consanguinity of one or more of the transferors.

8. between spouses resulting from a decree of dissolution of marriage or a decree of legal separation or from a property settlement agreement incidental to such a decree.

9. to or from any governmental entity.

10. transfers of new residences of not more than one dwelling unit which have not previously been occupied for residential purposes.

11. transfers of real property where the value of any dwelling does not exceed five percent of the value of the property. (*Note: This provision typically excludes a ranch or farm sale.*)

When the parties check the appropriate box in Section 7B, the parties define whether:

- the buyer has received the notice.
- the seller has a defined number of days to furnish it.
- the property is exempt from the requirement pursuant to the Texas Property Code.

There is no duty to disclose some types of specific information, according to this section of the code and Section 15E of the TRELA.

Subsection (c) of 5.008

(c) A seller or seller's agent shall have no duty to make a disclosure or release information related to whether a death by natural causes, suicide, or accident unrelated to the condition of the property occurred on the property or whether a previous occupant had, may have had, has, or may have AIDS, HIV-related illnesses, or HIV infection.

8. Brokers' Fees

Broker fees are not an issue between the seller and buyer, but rather between the seller and the listing broker and the buyer and the buyer's broker. In the case of a subagent, it is an issue for the listing broker and the selling broker. Commission splits between salespeople and the brokers who sponsor them must be defined by their employment or independent contractor agreement.

9. Closing

Closing the real estate transaction is the final step on the path that began with getting the listing. The **closing process** includes signing documents that transfer title of the property from the seller to the buyer and distribution of funds. Section 9 specifies the actual closing date for the sales transaction. The closing takes place on that particular date or before the date specified in this section. This section further explains the actions that take place during the closing, such as the delivery of the deed.

TEXAS LAW OF CONTRACTS

A. The closing of the sale will be on or before June 30, 20xx, . . .

10. Possession

Section 10 specifies that the buyer is given possession of the property at the closing date. If the seller is unable to move out after the closing, then a landlord and tenant relationship is created. This requires both parties to complete a lease agreement form promulgated by TREC.

☑ **upon closing and funding**

11. Special Provisions

Section 11 allows both parties to add any factual statements or business details relating to the sales contract. If several provisions exist and they exceed the space provided on the form, the parties may need to seek legal assistance.

Items that may be added to this section

- Inventory list
- Preclosing walk-through inspection
- Documents available for review prior to closing
- Who will pay for specific costs that may be incurred

Items that may not be addressed in this section

- The transaction is contingent upon the sale of another property.
- The contract is in a second or back-up position.
- The assumption transaction is contingent upon the seller's release of liability or, in the case of a VA guaranteed loan, restoration or VA entitlement.
- Arrangements for the buyer to possess before closing or the seller to stay after closing.
- The contract is contingent upon satisfactory inspections to the buyer.
- The parties agree that in the event of a dispute they will try mediation before bringing a lawsuit.
- Any wording that defines legal rights and remedies, such as "contingent upon, terminate, refund earnest money on demand, cancel, etc."
- "Time is of the essence" (parties should contact an attorney).

12. Settlement and Other Expenses

Section 12 contains the allocation of costs to complete the sales transaction between the buyer and the seller.

Seller's Expenses

- Prepayment penalties if applicable
- Recording fees
- Deed preparation fees
- Escrow fees

Buyer's Expenses

- Fees in connection with obtaining third party financing (credit report fees, impounds, underwriting, loan origination, discount points, etc.).
- Escrow fees
- Private mortgage insurance (PMI) in cash at closing or it may be added to the amount of the loan. Before you try to address this item, get help from the buyer's loan officer.

If any expense exceeds an amount set as a maximum in the contract, a party may terminate the contract unless the other party agrees to pay the excess.

(b) Seller shall not pay an amount not to exceed $1000 . . .

Sections 13, 14, 15, 17, 18, 19, 20 do not need to be completed. However, they must be read and understood by all parties.

13. Prorations

Section 13 clarifies that taxes, interest, maintenance fees, assessments, dues, and rents are prorated through the closing date.

14. Casualty Loss

Section 14 explains that if any part of the property is damaged or destroyed by fire or other disaster after the effective date of the contract, the seller must restore the property to its previous condition.

15. Default

Section 15 explains that if the buyer fails to comply with the contract, the buyer will be in **default**, and the seller may enforce specific performance, pursue other relief, or terminate the contract and receive the earnest money as damages.

16. Mediation

Section 16 states that all parties to the sales transaction are entitled to seek **mediation.** Mediation is a forum in which a neutral person, the mediator, facilitates communication between the parties and helps them resolve a dispute. You may encourage clients to seek mediation by highlighting the benefits of it, but you may not compel them to seek it.

☑ **will be submitted to a mutually acceptable . . .**

17. Attorney's Fees

Section 17 of the contract explains that all parties to a transaction are entitled to recover reasonable attorney's fees incurred by the prevailing party.

18. Escrow

An **escrow** is a small and short-lived trust arrangement during which time the paperwork required for the sale of real property is processed. The **escrow holder** (escrow company) acts as a neutral agent for both the buyer and seller. This section states that the parties give the escrow holder the authority to release the earnest money to the appropriate party. Both parties to the sales contract also agree not to hold the escrow holder liable when disbursing the earnest money.

19. Representations

Section 19 states that the seller assures that there are no other liens, assessments, or interests in the property that will not be satisfied from the sale proceeds. This section offers the buyer the option to terminate the sales contract if unexpected encumbrances arise.

20. Federal Tax Requirements

When the transaction closing takes place at a title company, the escrow agent ensures that IRS regulations are followed. Section 20 suggests that the parties to the transaction read and understand the paragraph and seek a professional if they have any questions.

21. Notices

Section 21 confirms the contact information for both parties and clarifies where special notices regarding the sales contract are to be sent. Correspondence between the parties must be in writing. Correspondence becomes effective once it has been mailed, hand-delivered, or transmitted by fax.

To Buyer at:
Sam and Cindy Winter
123 Triangle Square
Geometry, TX 76543
Telephone: (214) 000-0000
Facsimile: (214) 000-001
E-mail: thewinters@geometry.xyz

To Seller at:
Fred and Jan Spring
1652 Hill Street
Big City, TX 70000
Telephone: (806) 000-0000
Facsimile: (806) 000-0001
E-mail: thesprings@bigcity.xyz

22. Agreement of the Parties

Section 22 gives the parties an opportunity to disclose certain addenda that accompany the contract. **Addenda** represent forms that disclose additional information relating to the transaction. If certain addenda need to be attached to the sales contract, the agent should use the forms promulgated by TREC that relate to the situation. For example, if the buyer will assume the seller's loan, then an agent should utilize a Loan Assumption Addendum from TREC.

Addendums not to be listed in this section

- Seller's Disclosure Notice
- Information About Brokerage Services
- TAR Form - "Notification of Intermediary Relationship"

☑ **Third Party Financing Condition Addendum**
☑ **Addendum for Property Subject to Mandatory Membership in an Owners' Association**

23. Termination Option

In section 23 the termination option allows the buyer to terminate the sales contract and be free from any obligations to perform under the contract. Below are the provisions under the termination option.

Provisions

- The buyer may exercise the termination option for any reason and is not obligated to give a reason why they are terminating the contract.

- There is no option until the buyer pays the termination fee to the seller. When the seller accepts the terms and the option fee, the final page of the sales contract will acknowledge the receipt of the option fee.

- When choosing to exercise the option fee, time is of the essence. Therefore, the buyer has two days to exercise the option. The buyer may specify the number of days that the termination option will stand. The start date of the option begins on the effective date of the sales contract and continues until midnight of the day the option period ends.

- Both parties can agree to either credit the termination option fee as part of the sales price or not.

- To exercise the right to terminate, the buyer must complete a Notice of Termination of Contract form promulgated by TREC and then deliver it to the seller.

24. Consult an Attorney

Section 24 states that a real estate licensee does not have the authorization to provide legal counsel to a client. If the client has questions that require legal knowledge, refer him or her to an attorney. If the client has questions regarding the execution of the sales contract, he or she should consult an attorney prior to signing the agreement.

Broker Information and Ratification of Fee

This section contains the agreed upon commission split between the brokers of a sales transaction, as well as the contact information for the listing broker and any other brokers involved in the sale.

Listing broker has agreed to pay 2.5% of the total sales price

Buyer's Broker (Other Broker):
First Real Estate, License Number 000001 representing buyer as buyer's agent
Linda Rose, associate
123 4th Street
Walker, TX 70002
Telephone: (214) 111-1111
Facsimile: (214) 111-1112
E-mail: lrose@firstrealestate.xyz

Listing Broker:
Sunshine Real Estate, License Number 000002 representing seller
only as seller's agent
Pat Green, listing and selling associate
567 8th Street
Freedom, TX 70001
Telephone: (806) 765-4321
Facsimile: (806) 123-4568
E-mail: pgreen@sunshinere.xyz

Option Fee Receipt

If the buyer chooses for a termination option in Section 23, this section acts as the receipt of funds for that option. The seller or listing broker signs and dates this section to acknowledge receipt of the funds.

Receipt of $150 via personal check

Contract and Earnest Money Receipt

This section discloses that the escrow agent received the sales contract as well as the earnest money from the buyer.

Receipt of contract and earnest money in the amount of $5000 via personal check. Received by:
Any Title Company
321 Closing Avenue
Title, TX 76543
Telephone (000) 000-0000
Facsimile (000) 000-0001
E-mail: escrow@anytitle.xyz

Other Sales Contracts

The One To Four Family Residential Contract (Resale) is the most common sales contract, however five additional sales contracts are also used in Texas. The type of real estate involved in the sales transaction determines which contract is used. While the other sales contracts mirror the more common One To Four Family Residential Contract (Resale), there are a few key differences in the form itself. A real estate licensee in Texas should be alert to these differences when filling out the other sales contract forms.

Residential Condominium Contract (Resale)

Sales transactions involving a condominium form of ownership utilize the Residential Condominium Contract (Resale) form. In Texas, condominium sales transactions usually involve residential apartment buildings located in downtown, urban areas. The condominium form of ownership has recently gained popularity as Texas real estate expands. Each owner of a condominium holds title to his or her particular unit and shares common areas within the development, such as a pool or clubhouse. An owners' association manages the property and governs a condominium development with its own bylaws.

The Residential Condominium Contract (Resale) is essentially similar to a standard sales contract for a one to four family property. The primary difference is that the property description in Section 2 calls for the unit number, the building name, and the condominium project where the unit is located. Section 2 also contains information on the buyers obtaining a copy of the owners' association bylaws. It is important for the buyer to review the bylaws before signing the contract. Condominium sales transactions also require a TREC Condominium Resale Certificate. The Condominium Resale Certificate contains specific information regarding the owners' association, such as membership dues, special assessments, insurance, and an operating budget.

New Home Contract (Incomplete Construction)

New developments that are still under construction require a sales transaction that typically involves a New Home Contract (Incomplete Construction) form. Because the property did not physically exist at the time of the contract, the exclusion of detailed improvements in Section 2 is the primary difference in this form. Section 7 is also slightly different from the traditional One To Four Family Contract (Resale). Section 7 provides for information regarding the property construction and completion dates, insulation on the property, and the seller's disclosures regarding the incomplete property.

New Home Contract (Completed Construction)

A New Home Contract (Completed Construction) form refers to purchases in new developments where the property has already been constructed. For the most part, the contract form is similar to the One To Four Family Residential Contract (Resale). However, Section 2 does not contain detailed information because it is a new property, and Section 7 includes provisions regarding the buyer's acceptance of the property's present condition. Section 7 also contains references to any warranties that accompany the construction of the completed property as well as information regarding the property's insulation.

Unimproved Property Contract

When purchasing raw land where an improvement is absent from the property, parties to this transaction will involve an Unimproved Property Contract. This form is also similar to the One To Four Family Residential Contract (Resale), but because no physical structure rests on the land, Section 2 will not contain a comprehensive list of property details, and Section 7 will exclude information regarding structural improvements.

Farm and Ranch Contract

The Farm and Ranch Contract is used for transactions that involve property primarily used for agricultural purposes. Section 2 of the contract discloses information regarding the property description and any structures or accessories included with the sale. Unlike the One to Four Family Residential Contract (Resale), Section 2 in this form is tailored to improvements that are common to agricultural property, such as windmills, barns, and animal corrals. A subsection in Section 2 refers to the seller's right to harvest growing crops until actual possession of the property transfers to the new owner. Section 6 contains references to **exception documents** or any documentation that reveals information affecting title to real property. If any leases exist on the property, the seller must provide the buyer with copies of the lease contracts. Section 7 contains additional seller disclosures and a subsection allowing for the disclosure of the property subject to any government programs.

Summary

Within real estate sales, the **purchase agreement** is one of the most important contracts. The purchase agreement, or sales contract form, sets the terms of the sale of real property between the buyer and the seller.

Important elements when creating a valid sales contract include the **offer** and **acceptance**, **earnest money**, and **equitable title**. The offer and acceptance means that the buyer and seller must mutually agree to the terms of the sale. Earnest money is a cash down payment that solidifies a buyer's intent to honor the terms of the sales contract. Equitable title occurs when a buyer holds an interest in property that is legally vested in another person's name.

A Texas real estate broker or salesperson encounters the **One To Four Family Residential Contract (Resale)** regularly. It is a sales contract form promulgated by the Texas Real Estate Commission for residential property. Texas has different variations of this sales contract depending on the type of property for sale. Separate versions of the residential contract exist for transactions that involve condominiums or commercial property.

When filling out the contract form, be sure to have a thorough understanding of the different sections and be able to explain each section to the client.

Unit 7

Purchase Agreement Addenda

Introduction

The residential purchase agreement alone may not cover all terms of sale between a buyer and a seller. Therefore, it is sometimes necessary to attach an addendum, or addenda, to include any special conditions or terms that affect the sale of real property. An **addendum** is a separate document that is made part of a contract, by agreement of both parties. This unit covers various types of addenda forms promulgated by the Texas Real Estate Commission (TREC) and the content of each.

Learning Objectives

After reading this unit, you should be able to:

- explain the use of addenda in a sales contract.
- identify different types of addenda.
- describe the content of each addenda.

Addenda in Real Estate Contracts

As you previously learned, a buyer and seller of real property are bound to a purchase agreement contract. The most common type of this contract in Texas is the One To Four Family Residential Contract. It collects basic information and then prompts the licensee in Section 22 to add an addendum, or addenda, if needed to cover additional information that may affect the terms of the transaction, such as business details.

Basic Requirements

An agent must use an addendum form promulgated by TREC if such a form exists for the particular type of contingency. For example, if a buyer must sell his or her current home before purchasing another home, the agent can attach an Addendum for Sale of Other Property by Buyer form.

An addendum must reference the original contract of sale and be dated and signed by both parties.

There is a space in Section 11 of the One To Four Family Residential Contract that allows the parties to specify other changes to a contract that does not have an addendum. In no case shall the agent add anything in this section without the consent of the seller or buyer, as that would make the agent an attorney under TREC laws and the agent would be open to disciplinary action under TREC.

Contingencies

Addenda are frequently used to cover contingencies. A **contingency** is a requirement that something must occur before the goal of the contract—the property sale—can occur. When a contingency is added to a contract of sale, there is an implied promise that the requesting party will attempt to fulfill the contingency. When all contingencies of a contract are fulfilled, a buyer is obligated to complete the purchase.

Buyers often add one or more contingencies to a contract of sale. For example, a buyer may want to make the purchase contingent on the sale of another property.

Sellers may also insert contingencies. If a buyer adds contingencies to a contract of sale, a seller may add a statement to the contract that allows the property to continue to be marketed between the time of the offer and the closing.

A well-written contingency should reach completion before the closing date. All involved parties should be able to determine when a well-written contingency is fulfilled. An example of a poorly written contingency is a purchase made contingent upon finding a better home in the same area but for less money.

Disclosures

Addenda to a purchase agreement are also used to make **disclosures**, which reveal known facts. For example, sellers of previously occupied single-family residences must disclose material facts about the physical condition of the property.

Promulgated Addendum Forms

Below is a list of common promulgated forms that the Texas Real Estate Commission requires for specific contingencies. Real estate licensees should become familiar with the most common addenda that can accompany a sales contract.

Addendum for Sale of Other Property by Buyer

A buyer will often put a contingency in the contract of sale stating that the purchase of the new home is contingent on the sale of buyer's present home. This is because, if the seller accepts the buyer's offer to purchase, the buyer will have to make mortgage payments on the new home and most buyers cannot afford to make mortgage payments on both the new home and the present home.

If you have a buyer client in this situation, just complete and attach an **Addendum for Sale of Other Property by Buyer** to the residential sales contract to note this contingency. It is not uncommon for the combination of this contingency and the expiration date of the contract of sale to motivate a buyer to lower the sale price of his or her present home in order to sell it before his or her offer on the new home expires.

Section A of this addendum makes the sales contract contingent upon the buyer receiving the proceeds of the sale from his or her current property. A predetermined date for the sale of the property is specified and if the buyer is unable to sell the property by that date, then the sales contract will terminate. Failing to sell the property by that date will also entitle the buyer to recover the full amount of the earnest money.

Section B states that if a seller accepts a written backup offer to purchase the property, he or she must notify the buyer of the acceptance. Acceptance of the backup offer also requires that a buyer waive the contingency to sell his or her property. If the buyer elects to waive this contingency, he or she must continue honoring the terms of the sale and have the proceeds available to complete the purchase regardless if the buyer has actually sold their property or not. Typically, the buyer has five to seven days to waive the contingency. If he or she do not, the contract terminates and the buyer is given back the earnest money.

Section C requires the buyer to deposit additional earnest money if he or she elect to waive the contingency to sell the property. In addition, he or she must notify the seller that he or she is waiving the contingency.

Section D of this addendum states that if a buyer waives the Contingency, the buyer is in default if the buyer fails to close the transaction because of non-receipt of expected proceeds from the sale of the buyer's property. If the buyer defaults, the seller can obtain liquidated damages for breach of contract.

Section E states that time is of the essence and the terms of the addendum must be performed according to the dates specified.

Addendum for "Back-Up" Contract

An **Addendum for "Back-Up" Contract** states that a back-up contract serves as a replacement for the termination of a previous contract. Neither party is required to adhere to the terms of a back-up contract until the first contract terminates. However, the buyer of a back-up contract must still provide earnest money as well as any option fees. The addendum specifies the date that the back-up contract is contingent upon with respect to the performance of the first contract. If the first contract terminates before the specified date, the back-up contract goes into effect. If the first contract does not terminate, then the back-up contract terminates and the buyer will be refunded his or her earnest money deposit. In this particular addendum, time is of the essence and the provisions of the addendum must be performed based on the specified dates.

Release of Liability on Assumed Loan and/or Restoration of Seller's VA Entitlement

This addendum states that the seller wants to be released from liability on an assumed loan. The assumed loan can be either a conventional loan or a government loan. The addendum provides that the buyer must obtain approval from the lender for the loan assumption before the closing date. If the loan assumption and release of liability has not been approved by the closing date, if Box A(1) is checked the contract terminates and the earnest money will be returned to the buyer. If Box A(2) is checked, the buyer can continue to work on the release of liability after the closing.

The addendum also concerns a transaction in which a seller originally obtained a loan from the Veterans Administration. If the seller wishes to purchase a home utilizing the benefits under the Veterans Administration, this addendum gives the seller time to restore these VA entitlements. The seller will pay any costs incurred securing the release of liability and restoration of VA entitlement. If the seller cannot obtain restoration of the VA entitlements by the closing date, then he or she can terminate the contract or proceed with the transaction.

TEXAS LAW OF CONTRACTS

Seller's Temporary Residential Lease

The **Seller's Temporary Residential Lease** applies if a seller remains on the property after the sales transaction closes; he or she becomes a tenant of the buyer under a lease agreement. This addendum carries out the provisions of a lease agreement, which is similar to the more common lease agreement form promulgated by the Texas Association of REALTORS®.

Under this addendum, the buyer is already in possession of title to the property, but the seller remains on the property. The buyer and the seller have the freedom to negotiate the specifics of the lease agreement under this addendum. If the seller intends to remain on the property for more than 90 days, this addendum cannot be used and a more comprehensive lease agreement must be drafted.

Buyer's Temporary Residential Lease

The **Buyer's Temporary Residential Lease** is the opposite of the Seller's Temporary Residential Lease. If the buyer occupies the property for sale prior to closing, he or she becomes a tenant of the seller under a lease agreement. The major difference is that the termination date of the temporary lease agreement can vary.

The termination date can be the:

- date of closing.
- termination of the contract prior to the closing date.
- default of the lease agreement by the buyer/tenant.
- default of the sales contract by the buyer/tenant.

A seller should take cautionary measures when allowing a buyer to occupy a property before the closing of a sales transaction. In the event that the buyer is unable to complete the transaction and does not vacate the property, the seller may have to utilize the eviction process. The eviction process may cause unnecessary delays for the seller and stall the sale of the property.

Seller Financing Addendum

A purchase agreement can include a **Seller Financing Addendum** that allows the seller to assist the purchase of the property by offering the buyer a loan payable with interest. This addendum compares the specific details of this financing arrangement with the purchase agreement.

Section A of the addendum states that the buyer must provide the following for adequate credit documentation:

- a credit report.
- verification of employment with salary history.
- verification of available funds in financial institutions.
- a current financial statement that establishes the buyer's creditworthiness.

This information must be presented to the seller within a specified number of days after the effective date of the contract.

Section B states if the seller does not receive the credit documentation from the buyer, the seller can terminate the contract then and receive the earnest money 7 days after the specified time of delivery. If the seller receives the credit documentation on time, but does not approve of the buyer's credit, the seller can terminate the contract within 7 days and the buyer will retain the earnest money. This section also states that if a seller does not terminate the contract after reviewing the buyer's credit, the seller is deemed to have accepted the buyer's credit.

Section C contains the terms of the promissory note that the seller will offer to the buyer, such as the amount of each payment, the length of the terms, the interest rate, and the balance due. The terms specified in this section will vary based on the financing arrangement that is chosen.

Section D covers the terms of the deed of trust securing the promissory note. A property can be sold with or without the consent of the seller if the new buyer assumes the existing note or the full balance on the note is paid respectively. This section also gives the option of whether an escrow will be used to collect taxes and insurance.

TEXAS LAW OF CONTRACTS

Addendum for Coastal Area Property

The **Addendum for Coastal Area Property** refers to a transaction that involves property that adjoins tidewaters. To the prospective buyer, this means that the nature of the water next to the property can change naturally. Therefore, the natural tendency for the tide to flood or recede can either add or remove portions of the property. The addendum also covers other legal aspects concerning the use of property next to tidewaters. If the seller's property is located near tidewaters and he or she fails to include this addendum, the buyer can terminate the contract and retrieve his or her earnest money.

Addendum for Property Located Seaward of the Gulf Intracoastal Waterway

This addendum refers to real property in a sales transaction that is located seaward of the Gulf Intracoastal Waterway. Property near this waterway is subject to a public easement and prevents the property owner from interfering with the easement. If this addendum applies to the property for sale and the seller fails to disclose this information, a buyer can terminate the contract and retrieve his or her earnest money.

Addendum for Property Subject to Mandatory Membership in an Owners' Association

This addendum is in reference to property that is sold and is subject to a mandatory membership in an owners' association. Typically, common interest properties like planned unit developments are subject to the operation of a homeowners' association. The association is responsible for the maintenance of the common interest elements of the property and creates bylaws within the development regarding the use of the property. This addendum allows the buyer to obtain information from the seller regarding the owners' association.

Section A of the addendum specifies the manner in which the information will be disseminated to the buyer. The information can be delivered to the buyer after a specific number of days, which allows the buyer to terminate the contract and have the earnest money returned to him or her if the information is not received by that time. Other options in this section state that the buyer already received and approved the owners' association information or that the buyer does not wish to view the association information. If the buyer does not wish to obtain the information, then he or she waives the right to terminate the contract.

Section B discloses the amount of association fees that are a result of the transfer of ownership from the seller to the buyer.

Subdivision Information, Including Resale Certificate for Property Subject to Mandatory Membership in an Owners' Association

This addendum is used in connection with the aforementioned 36-5 addendum. When the buyer requests information regarding the owners' association, this form is used to provide more details, such as association fees, special assessments, capital expenditures, compliance with governmental regulations, and general information about the owners' association.

Notice of Termination of Contract

If a buyer opts to terminate the sales contract, this addendum provides notice to the seller. The **Notice of Termination of Contract** addendum form exercises the buyer's unrestricted right to terminate a sales contract.

Amendment

Should either party to the contract of sale wish to change an existing element of the contract, they may do so as long as it is agreeable to the other party. This type of change is referred to as an **amendment** or **novation**. If the buyer or seller wishes to make amendments to the sales contract, they can utilize this form. Numbered sections of the form constitute different items in the sales contract that the buyer and seller may agree to modify. Any other amendments that are pertinent to the sales contract but do not appear in the numbered sections can be included in Section 9 of this addendum.

Third Party Financing Condition Addendum

Third party financing refers to the securing of funds from an outside source in order to finance a purchase. The **Third Party Financing Condition Addendum** describes in detail the nature of the financing that the buyer will obtain. Typically, this is accomplished by obtaining a loan from a mortgage lender.

Section A of this addendum refers to obtaining a loan through conventional financing. A **conventional loan** is any loan made by lenders without any governmental guarantees. Institutional lenders that provide conventional financing include commercial banks, savings and loan associations, credit unions, and life insurance companies. This section also outlines the type of conventional financing the buyer will seek and the terms of the loan.

Sections B, C, and D refer to a buyer seeking a loan through government financing. Two federal agencies and one state agency help make it possible for people to buy a home they would never be able to purchase without government involvement. The two federal agencies that participate in real estate financing are the Federal Housing Administration (FHA) and the Veterans Administration (VA). The FHA does not make loans; rather, it insures lenders against loss. Authorized lending institutions, such as banks, savings banks, and independent mortgage companies make loans. As long as FHA guidelines are used in funding the loan, the FHA, upon default by the borrower, insures the lender against loss. The Texas Veterans Housing Assistance Program (VHAP) is a state program that helps eligible veterans obtain loans at a lower than market interest rate. The Veterans Administration does not make loans, but like the FHA, it guarantees loans made by an approved institutional lender. Sections C and D also state the terms of the government financing.

Loan Assumption Addendum

Financing through assumption refers to the buyer seeking to assume the seller's existing loan. When the buyer assumes the seller's loan, the buyer becomes responsible for repayment of the loan as well as any other obligations to the lender. The **Loan Assumption Addendum** provides the details regarding this type of transaction.

Section A of the addendum states that the buyer assuming the loan must provide the following for adequate credit documentation:

- a credit report.
- verification of employment with salary history.
- verification of available funds in financial institutions.
- a current financial statement.
- any other information that establishes the buyer's creditworthiness.

This information must also be presented to the seller within a specified number of days after the effective date of the contract.

Section B establishes that if the seller does not receive the credit documentation from the buyer, the seller can terminate the contract and receive the earnest money after 7 days from the specified time of delivery. If the seller receives the credit documentation on time, but does not approve of the buyer's credit, the seller can terminate the contract within 7 days and the buyer will retain the earnest money. Furthermore, this section also states that if a seller does not terminate the contract after reviewing the buyer's credit, they are under the assumption that they approved the buyer's credit.

Section C contains the unpaid balance as well as the monthly payments to the specified lien holder for the first promissory note and the second promissory note if applicable. Under this section, the buyer's first payment will be the first payment after the closing date and the buyer agrees to assume all obligations under the promissory note.

Careful consideration should be given to the unpaid balance of the loan. If the actual unpaid balance of the loan varies by more than $350 at the closing, the buyer or seller can opt to terminate the contract unless one party agrees to pay the difference. Obtaining the most recent payoff statement from the mortgage lender will help prevent any discrepancies in the loan balance.

This addendum also provides a space that discloses the maximum amount for the assumption fee. If the lender requires an assumption fee that is greater than the one stated in the addendum, the seller must pay the difference. If the seller does not agree to pay the difference, the buyer can terminate the contract and retrieve the earnest money. This also applies to any changes in the terms of the loan, such as the interest rate or the type of loan, prior to the closing.

Although the buyer assumes the loan, the seller will still be held liable to the lender for timely payments unless the lender chooses to administer a release of liability. In order to protect a seller without a release of liability, a vendor's lien and deed of trust are used in the event that the buyer misses a payment and defaults on the loan. If a buyer fails to make a payment, the vendor's lien and deed of trust gives the seller the right to repossess title to the property.

Notices to both the buyer and seller are at the end of this addendum. The notice to the buyer states that the terms of the loan may be subject to adjustment after the closing. A buyer should review the loan documents carefully or have an attorney examine them for possible adjustments. The notice to the seller reiterates the fact that the seller will remain liable for the loan unless he or she obtains a release of liability from the lender or utilizes a Release of Liability Addendum.

Notice to Prospective Buyer

An abstract of title is a summary of recorded documents that contains information that may affect title to real property. The **Notice To Prospective Buyer Addendum** advises the buyer to obtain legal counsel from an attorney to examine the abstract of title. The addendum also states that if the property purchased is located in a utility district, the seller must provide the buyer a statutory notice disclosing the tax rate, bonded indebtedness, or standby fee of the district. The buyer must then sign the addendum to signify that he or she received a copy of the notice.

Summary

Frequently a residential purchase agreement alone will not cover all terms of the sale between a buyer and a seller. As a result, it is often necessary to include an **addendum** or addenda that state(s) any special conditions that affect the sale of real property. An addendum is added to the contract based upon the agreement of the buyer and the seller. A real estate licensee must use an addendum form promulgated by TREC if such a form exists. Common addenda cover a wide range of things, including sale of other property by buyer, seller financing, and leasing of the residence.

A **contingency** is a requirement that something must occur before the sale of the property—the goal of the contract—can occur. When a contingency is added to a contract of sale, there is an implied promise that the requesting party will attempt to fulfill the contingency. Both buyers and sellers can include contingencies in a contract of sale.

A well-written contingency should be complete before the closing date. All involved parties should also be able to determine when a well-written contingency is fulfilled.

Unit 8

Lease Agreements

Introduction

One of the rights included in owning real property is the right to lease the property. If a property owner chooses to lease the property, he or she may want to state the terms of the lease in a contract. This unit defines lease agreements and explains each section of the residential lease agreement form. In order to understand the nature of a lease, you must understand the basics of leasing real estate and the different types of leasehold estates, also explained in this unit.

Learning Objectives

After reading this unit, you should be able to:

- define a lease of real property.
- list the requirements of a valid lease.
- identify different types of leasehold estates.
- summarize the sections in a residential lease agreement.

Defining a Lease

A **lease** is a contract in which a property owner offers a proposed tenant the right to occupy the property for a specific amount of time. The property owner leasing the property is considered the **lessor**, or landlord. The tenant is known as the **lessee**. The lessor maintains a **reversionary right**, meaning that the property reverts to the lessor when the lease expires.

Requirements of a Valid Lease

Creating a valid lease is similar to creating a contract. One difference is that, according to the Statute of Frauds, a lease for more than one year must be in writing. A lease agreement with a duration of less than one year may be made orally, but a landlord usually prefers such a lease to be written. The requirements of a valid lease are as follows:

1. **Legal competency of parties** - The parties to a lease must have the mental capacity to contract.

2. **Mutual consent** - An offer and acceptance of the lease agreement must be established with genuine assent.

3. **Lawful objective** - The lease agreement must not violate the law.

4. **Consideration** - A lease agreement states that the tenant obtains the right to occupy the property in return for rent payment.

5. **Legal description** - The property offered for rent must be described.

When determining the validity of a lease, Texas courts will apply contract rules. A lease will usually be found to be valid if it indicates the intent of one person to convey temporary possession of a specific piece of realty to another person.

Types of Leasehold Estates

A **leasehold estate** constitutes the tenant's right to occupy the property under the terms of a lease agreement. The different types of leasehold estates are an estate for years, a periodic estate, a tenancy at will, and a tenancy at sufferance.

Estate for Years

An **estate for years** is a type of leasehold estate that runs for a specific duration. Whether it runs from month to month, week to week, or year to year, an estate for years has a definite beginning and end. An estate for years does not automatically renew and once the lease expires, the tenant must vacate the property and possession reverts to the lessor. If the tenant wishes to continue occupying the property, he or she must sign a new lease agreement or, sometimes, depending on the terms, the lease can convert to a periodic estate.

Periodic Estates

A **periodic estate** is a type of leasehold estate that occurs when the tenant and the landlord agree to a lease without a specified expiration date and the lease runs indefinitely. The payment of rent takes place at specific intervals during the lease, such as every month or every two weeks. The lease agreement specifically outlines when the payment of rent will occur.

Unlike an estate for years, a periodic estate will automatically renew until one of the parties decides to terminate the lease agreement. As stated earlier, depending on the terms of the lease agreement, a leasehold estate can begin as an estate for years and then convert to a periodic estate when the lease expires.

Tenancy at Will

A **tenancy at will** is a leasehold estate that lasts until the lessor or lessee terminates the lease agreement. Like the periodic estate, a tenancy at will can run indefinitely, but will only continue to do so at the lessor or lessee's consent. A tenancy at will can also terminate by the death of either party. Similar to the aforementioned leasehold estate, a tenancy at will allows a tenant to occupy the property while the landlord receives rent payments.

Tenancy at Sufferance

A **tenancy at sufferance** occurs when a tenant continues to occupy a leased property after a lease has expired. In this case, the tenant is occupying the property without the landlord's consent. As a result, the landlord may choose to pursue the eviction process in order to remove the tenant.

Residential Lease Agreement Form

As discussed earlier, the Statute of Frauds in Texas calls for lease agreements to be in writing if the lease is for more than one year. However, landlords will generally call for all lease agreements to be in writing regardless of the duration. This is done to protect the landlord and the tenant if legal arbitration is necessary. Originally, lease agreements were created to protect the landlord only. Texas has since passed the **Landlord and Tenant Act**, which is a statute under the Texas Property Code that addresses the rights of both the landlord and the tenant in a lease agreement.

A common lease agreement form in Texas is the Residential Lease created by the Texas Association of REALTORS®. Only members of the Texas Association of REALTORS® can utilize this form.

TEXAS ASSOCIATION OF REALTORS®
RESIDENTIAL LEASE
USE OF THIS FORM BY PERSONS WHO ARE NOT MEMBERS OF THE TEXAS ASSOCIATION OF REALTORS® IS NOT AUTHORIZED.
©Texas Association of REALTORS®, Inc. 2009

1. **PARTIES:** The parties to this lease are:

the owner of the Property, Landlord,: _____
_____; and

Tenant(s): _____
_____.

2. **PROPERTY:** Landlord leases to Tenant the following real property:

Address: _____
legally described as:_____
_____
in _____ County, Texas, together with the following non-real-property
items: _____
_____.

The real property and the non-real-property are collectively called the "Property".

3. **TERM:**

A. Primary Term: The primary term of this lease begins and ends as follows:

Commencement Date:_____ Expiration Date:_____.

B. Delay of Occupancy: Tenant must occupy the Property within 5 days after the Commencement Date. If Tenant is unable to occupy the Property by the 5th day after the Commencement Date because of construction on the Property or a prior tenant's holding over of the Property, Tenant may terminate this lease by giving written notice to Landlord before the Property becomes available to be occupied by Tenant, and Landlord will refund to Tenant the security deposit and any rent paid. Landlord will abate rent on a daily basis for a delay caused by construction or a prior tenant's holding over. This paragraph does not apply to any delay in occupancy caused by cleaning, repairs, or make-ready items.

4. **AUTOMATIC RENEWAL AND NOTICE OF TERMINATION:**

A. This lease automatically renews on a month-to-month basis unless Landlord or Tenant provides the other party <u>written</u> notice of termination not less than: *(Check only one box.)*
❑ (1) 30 days before the Expiration Date.
❑ (2) _____ days before the Expiration Date.

B. If this lease automatically renews on a month-to month basis, it will continue to renew on a month-to-month basis until either party provides <u>written</u> notice of termination to the other party and the notice of termination will be effective: *(Check only one box.)*
❑ (1) on the last day of the month following the month in which the notice is given. Landlord is not obligated to prorate rent even if Tenant surrenders the Property before the termination date.
❑ (2) on the date designated in the notice but not sooner than 30 days after the notice is given and, if necessary, rent will be prorated on a daily basis.

(TAR-2001) 8-25-09   Tenants:_____, _____, _____, _____ & Landlord or Landlord's Representative:_____, _____   Page 1 of 14

Residential Lease concerning:_____

   C. <u>Oral notice of termination is not sufficient under any circumstances</u>. Time is of the essence for providing notice of termination (strict compliance with dates by which notice must be provided is required). If a box is not checked under Paragraph 4A, Paragraph 4A(1) will apply. If a box is not checked under Paragraph 4B, Paragraph 4B(1) will apply.

5. RENT:

   A. <u>Monthly Rent</u>: Tenant will pay Landlord monthly rent in the amount of $_____ for each full month during this lease. The first full month's rent is due and payable not later than _____.
Thereafter, Tenant will pay the monthly rent so that Landlord receives the monthly rent on or before:
   ❏ (1) the first day of each month during this lease.
   ❏ (2) _____.
       Weekends, holidays, and mail delays do not excuse Tenant's obligation to timely pay rent.

   B. <u>Prorated Rent</u>: On or before _____ Tenant will pay Landlord $_____ as prorated rent from the Commencement Date through the last day of the month in which this lease begins.

   C. <u>Place of Payment</u>: Unless this lease provides otherwise, Tenant will remit all amounts due to Landlord under this lease to the following person or entity at the place stated and make all payments payable to the named person or entity. Landlord may later designate, in writing, another person or place to which Tenant must remit amounts due under this lease.
       Name: _____
       Address: _____
                    _____
            Notice: Place the Property address and Tenant's name on all payments.

   D. <u>Method of Payment</u>:
      (1) Tenant must pay all rent timely and without demand, deduction, or offset, except as permitted by law or this lease.
      (2) Time is of the essence for the payment of rent (strict compliance with rental due dates is required).
      (3) Unless the parties agree otherwise, Tenant may not pay rent in cash and will pay all rent by check, cashier's check, money order, or other means acceptable to Landlord.
      (4) Landlord ❏ requires ❏ does not require   Tenant(s) to pay monthly rents by one check or draft.
      (5) If Tenant fails to timely pay any amounts due under this lease or if any check of Tenant is not honored by the institution on which it was drawn, Landlord may require Tenant to pay such amount and any subsequent amounts under this lease in certified funds. This paragraph does not limit Landlord from seeking other remedies under this lease for Tenant's failure to make timely payments with good funds.

   E. <u>Rent Increases</u>: There will be no rent increases through the primary term. Landlord may increase the rent that will be paid during any month-to-month renewal period by providing at least 30 days written notice to Tenant.

6. LATE CHARGES:

   A. If Landlord does not <u>actually receive</u> a rent payment in the full amount at the designated place of payment by 11:59 p.m. on the _____ day *(insert a number of 1 or more)* <u>after</u> the date on which it is due according to Paragraph 5A, Tenant will pay Landlord for each late payment:
      (1) an initial late charge equal to *(check one box only)*: ❏ (a) $_____; or ❏ (b)_____% of one month's rent; **and**
      (2) additional late charges of $_____ per day thereafter until rent and late charges are paid in full. Additional late charges for any one payment may not exceed more than 30 days.

(TAR-2001) 8-25-09   Tenants:_____, _____, _____, _____ & Landlord or Landlord's Representative:_____, ____   Page 2 of 14

Residential Lease concerning:_____

B. For the purposes of paying rent and any late charges, the mailbox is not the agent for receipt for Landlord (the postmark date is not the date Landlord receives the payment). The parties agree that the late charge is based on a reasonable estimate of uncertain damages to the Landlord that are incapable of precise calculation and result from late payment of rent. Landlord's acceptance of a late charge does not waive Landlord's right to exercise remedies under Paragraph 27.

7. **RETURNED CHECKS:** Tenant will pay Landlord $_____ for each check Tenant tenders to Landlord which is returned or not honored by the institution on which it is drawn for any reason, plus any late charges until Landlord receives payment. Tenant must make any returned check good by paying such amount(s) plus any associated charges in certified funds.

8. **APPLICATION OF FUNDS:** Regardless of any notation on a check, Landlord may apply funds received from Tenant first to any non-rent obligations of Tenant, including but not limited to, late charges, returned check charges, repairs, brokerage fees, periodic utilities, pet charges, and then to rent.

9. **PETS:**

A. Unless the parties agree otherwise in writing, Tenant may not permit, even temporarily, any pet on the Property (including but not limited to any mammal, reptile, bird, fish, rodent, or insect).

B. If Tenant violates this Paragraph 9 or any agreement to keep a pet on the Property, Landlord may take all or any of the following action:
   (1) declare Tenant to be in default of this lease and exercise Landlord's remedies under Paragraph 27;
   (2) charge Tenant, as additional rent, an initial amount of $___ and $_____ per day thereafter per pet for each day Tenant violates the pet restrictions;
   (3) remove or cause to be removed any unauthorized pet and deliver it to appropriate local authorities by providing at least 24-hour written notice to Tenant of Landlord's intention to remove the unauthorized pet; and
   (4) charge to Tenant the Landlord's cost to:
      (a) remove any unauthorized pet;
      (b) exterminate the Property for fleas and other insects;
      (c) clean and deodorize the Property's carpets and drapes; and
      (d) repair any damage to the Property caused by the unauthorized pet.

C. When taking any action under Paragraph 9B Landlord will not be liable for any harm, injury, death, or sickness to any pet.

10. **SECURITY DEPOSIT:**

A. Security Deposit: On or before execution of this lease, Tenant will pay a security deposit to Landlord in the amount of $_____. "Security deposit" has the meaning assigned to that term in §92.102, Property Code.

B. Interest: No interest or income will be paid to Tenant on the security deposit. Landlord may place the security deposit in an interest-bearing or income-producing account and any interest or income earned will be paid to Landlord or Landlord's representative.

C. Refund: Tenant must give Landlord at least thirty (30) days written notice of surrender before Landlord is obligated to refund or account for the security deposit.

Notices about Security Deposits:
(1) §92.108, Property Code provides that a tenant may not withhold payment of any portion of the last month's rent on grounds that the security deposit is security for unpaid rent.

(TAR-2001) 8-25-09   Tenants:_____, _____, _____, _____ & Landlord or Landlord's Representative:_____, _____   Page 3 of 14

(2) Bad faith violations of §92.108 may subject a tenant to liability up to 3 times the rent wrongfully withheld and the landlord's reasonable attorney's fees.

(3) The Property Code does not obligate a landlord to return or account for the security deposit until the tenant surrenders the Property and gives the landlord a written statement of the tenant's forwarding address, after which the landlord has 30 days in which to account.

(4) "Surrender" is defined in Paragraph 16 of this lease.

(5) One may view the Texas Property Code at the Texas Legislature's website which, as of the date shown in the lower left-hand corner of this form, is http://tlo2.tlc.state.tx.us/statutes/pr.toc.htm.

D. Deductions:

    (1) Landlord may deduct reasonable charges from the security deposit for:

        (a) damages to the Property, excluding normal wear and tear, and all reasonable costs associated to repair the Property;

        (b) costs for which Tenant is responsible to clean, deodorize, exterminate, and maintain the Property;

        (c) unpaid or accelerated rent;

        (d) unpaid late charges;

        (e) unpaid utilities and utility expenses Landlord incurs to maintain utilities to the Property as required by this Lease;

        (f) unpaid pet charges;

        (g) replacing unreturned keys, garage door openers, security devices, or other components;

        (h) the removal of unauthorized locks or fixtures installed by Tenant;

        (i) Landlord's cost to access the Property if made inaccessible by Tenant;

        (j) missing or burned-out light bulbs and fluorescent tubes (at the same location and of the same type and quality that are in the Property on the Commencement Date);

        (k) packing, removing, and storing abandoned property;

        (l) removing abandoned or illegally parked vehicles;

        (m) costs of reletting (as defined in Paragraph 27), if Tenant is in default;

        (n) attorney's fees, costs of court, costs of service, and other reasonable costs incurred in any legal proceeding against Tenant;

        (o) mailing costs associated with sending notices to Tenant for any violations of this lease; and

        (p) any other unpaid charges or fees or other items for which Tenant is responsible under this lease.

    (2) If deductions exceed the security deposit, Tenant will pay to Landlord the excess within 10 days after Landlord makes written demand.

11. UTILITIES:

A. Tenant will pay all connection fees, service fees, usage fees, and all other costs and fees for all utilities to the Property (for example, electricity, gas, water, wastewater, garbage, telephone, alarm monitoring systems, cable, and Internet connections) except the following which Landlord will pay:_____

_____.

Unless otherwise agreed, amounts under this paragraph are payable directly to the service providers.

B. Unless provided by Landlord, Tenant must, at a minimum, keep the following utilities on, if available, at all times this lease is in effect: gas; electricity; water; wastewater; and garbage services.

Notice: Before signing this lease, Tenant should determine if all necessary utilities are available to the Property and are adequate for Tenant's use.

(TAR-2001) 8-25-09   Tenants:_____, _____, _____, _____ & Landlord or Landlord's Representative:_____, ____   Page 4 of 14

Residential Lease concerning:_____

12. USE AND OCCUPANCY:

A. <u>Occupants</u>: Tenant may use the Property as a private residence only. The only persons Tenant may permit to reside on the Property during the term of this lease are (*include names and ages of all occupants*): _____
_____
_____.

B. <u>Phone Numbers</u>: Tenant must promptly inform Landlord of any changes in Tenant's phone numbers (home, work, and mobile) not later than 5 days after a change.

C. <u>HOA Rules</u>: Tenant must comply with any owners' association rules or restrictive covenants affecting the Property. Tenant will reimburse Landlord for any fines or other charges assessed against Landlord for violations by Tenant of any owners' association rule or restrictive covenant.

D. <u>Prohibitions</u>: Unless otherwise authorized by this lease, Tenant may not install or permit any of the following on the Property, even temporarily: a spa, hot tub, above-ground pool, trampoline, or any item which causes a suspension or cancellation of insurance coverage or an increase in insurance premiums. Tenant may not permit any part of the Property to be used for: (1) any activity which is a nuisance, offensive, noisy, or dangerous; (2) the repair of any vehicle; (3) any business of any type, including but not limited to child care; (4) any activity which violates any zoning ordinance, owners' association rule, or restrictive covenant; (5) any illegal or unlawful activity; or (6) activity that obstructs, interferes with, or infringes on the rights of other persons near the Property.

E. <u>Guests</u>: Tenant may not permit any guest to stay on the Property longer the amount of time permitted by any owners' association rule or restrictive covenant or _____ days without Landlord's written permission, whichever is less.

F. <u>Common Areas</u>: Landlord is not obligated to pay any non-mandatory or user fees for Tenant's use of any common areas or facilities (for example, pool or tennis courts).

13. PARKING RULES: Tenant may not permit more than _____ vehicles, including but not limited to automobiles, trucks, recreational vehicles, trailers, motorcycles, all-terrain vehicles, jet skis, and boats, on the Property unless authorized by Landlord in writing. Tenant may not park or permit any person to park any vehicles in the yard. Tenant may permit vehicles to be parked only in drives, garages, designated common parking areas, or in the street if not prohibited by law or an owners' association. Tenant may not store or permit any person to store any vehicles on or adjacent to the Property or on the street in front of the Property. In accordance with applicable state and local laws, Landlord may have towed, at Tenant's expense: (a) any inoperative vehicle on or adjacent to the Property; (b) any vehicle parked in violation of this paragraph or any additional parking rules made part of this lease; or (c) any vehicle parked in violation of any law, local ordinance, or owners' association rule.

14. ACCESS BY LANDLORD:

A. <u>Advertising</u>: Landlord may prominently display a "For Sale" or "For Lease" or similarly worded sign on the Property during the term of this lease or any renewal period. Landlord or Landlord's contractor may take interior or exterior photographs or images of the Property and use the photographs or images in any advertisements to lease or sell the Property.

B. <u>Access</u>: Before accessing the Property, Landlord or anyone authorized by Landlord will attempt to first contact Tenant, but may enter the Property at reasonable times without notice to make repairs or to show the Property to prospective tenants or buyers, inspectors, fire marshals, lenders, appraisers, or insurance agents. Additionally, Landlord or anyone authorized by Landlord may peacefully enter the Property at reasonable times without first attempting to contact Tenant and without notice to: (1) survey

(TAR-2001) 8-25-09   Tenants:_____, _____, _____, _____ & Landlord or Landlord's Representative:_____, _____   Page 5 of 14

or review the Property's condition and take photographs to document the condition; (2) make emergency repairs; (3) exercise a contractual or statutory lien; (4) leave written notices; or (5) seize nonexempt property if Tenant is in default.

C. Trip Charges: If Landlord or Landlord's agents have made prior arrangements with Tenant to access the Property and are denied or are not able to access the Property because of Tenant's failure to make the Property accessible, Landlord may charge Tenant a trip charge of $_____.

D. Keybox: **A keybox is a locked container placed on the Property holding a key to the Property. The keybox is opened by a special combination, key, or programmed access device so that persons with the access device may enter the Property, even in Tenant's absence. The keybox is a convenience but involves risk (such as unauthorized entry, theft, property damage, or personal injury). Neither the Association of REALTORS® nor MLS requires the use of a keybox.**

    (1) Tenant authorizes Landlord, Landlord's property manager, and Landlord's broker to place on the Property a keybox containing a key to the Property:
        (a) during the last _____ days of this lease or any renewal or extension; and
        (b) at any time Landlord lists the Property for sale with a Texas licensed broker.

    (2) Tenant may withdraw Tenant's authorization to place a keybox on the Property by providing written notice to Landlord and paying Landlord a fee of $_____ as consideration for the withdrawal. Landlord will remove the keybox within a reasonable time after receipt of the notice of withdrawal and payment of the required fee. Removal of the keybox does not alleviate Tenant's obligation to make the Property available for showings as indicated in Paragraph 14B.

    (3) If Landlord or Landlord's agents have notified Tenant of their intent to access the Property to show it to prospects and are denied or are not able to access the Property because of Tenant's failure to make the Property accessible, Landlord may charge Tenant a trip charge of $_____.

    (4) Landlord, the property manager, and Landlord's broker are not responsible to Tenant, Tenant's guests, family, or occupants for any damages, injuries, or losses arising from use of the keybox unless caused by Landlord, the property manager, or Landlord's broker.

15. MOVE-IN CONDITION:

A. Landlord makes no express or implied warranties as to the Property's condition. Tenant has inspected the Property and accepts it **AS-IS** provided that Landlord:_____
_____
_____.

B. Tenant will complete an Inventory and Condition Form, noting any damages to the Property, and deliver it to Landlord within _____ days after the Commencement Date. If Tenant fails to timely deliver the Inventory and Condition Form, the Property will be deemed to be free of damages, unless otherwise expressed in this lease. The Inventory and Condition Form is not a request for repairs. Tenant must direct all requests for repairs in compliance with Paragraph 18.

16. MOVE-OUT:

A. Move-Out Condition: When this lease ends, Tenant will surrender the Property in the same condition as when received, normal wear and tear excepted. Tenant will leave the Property in a clean condition free of all trash, debris, and any personal property. Tenant may not abandon the Property.

B. Definitions:

    (1) "*Normal wear and tear*" means deterioration that occurs without negligence, carelessness, accident, or abuse.

(TAR-2001) 8-25-09   Tenants:_____, _____, _____, _____ & Landlord or Landlord's Representative:_____, _____   Page 6 of 14

Residential Lease concerning:_____

      (2) "*Surrender*" occurs when all occupants have vacated the Property, in Landlord's reasonable judgment, and one of the following events occurs:

          (a) the date Tenant specifies as the move-out or termination date in a written notice to Landlord has passed; or

          (b) Tenant returns keys and access devices that Landlord provided to Tenant under this lease.

      (3) "*Abandonment*" occurs when all of the following occur:

          (a) all occupants have vacated the Property, in Landlord's reasonable judgment;

          (b) Tenant is in breach of this lease by not timely paying rent; and

          (c) Landlord has delivered written notice to Tenant, by affixing it to the inside of the main entry door or if the Landlord is prevented from entering the Property by affixing it to the outside of the main entry door, stating that Landlord considers the Property abandoned, and Tenant fails to respond to the affixed notice by the time required in the notice, which will not be less than 2 days from the date the notice is affixed to the main entry door.

  C. Personal Property Left After Move-Out:

      (1) If Tenant leaves any personal property in the Property after surrendering or abandoning the Property Landlord may:

          (a) dispose of such personal property in the trash or a landfill;

          (b) give such personal property to a charitable organization; or

          (c) store and sell such personal property by following procedures in §54.045(b)-(e), Property Code.

      (2) Tenant must reimburse Landlord all Landlord's reasonable costs under Paragraph 16C(1) for packing, removing, storing, and selling the personal property left in the Property after surrender or abandonment.

17. PROPERTY MAINTENANCE:

  A. Tenant's General Responsibilities: Tenant, at Tenant's expense, must:

      (1)   keep the Property clean and sanitary;

      (2)   promptly dispose of all garbage in appropriate receptacles;

      (3)   supply and change heating and air conditioning filters at least once a month;

      (4)   supply and replace all light bulbs, fluorescent tubes, and batteries for smoke detectors, carbon monoxide detectors, garage door openers, ceiling fan remotes, and other devices (of the same type and quality that are in the Property on the Commencement Date);

      (5)   maintain appropriate levels of necessary chemicals or matter in any water softener;

      (6)   take action to promptly eliminate any dangerous condition on the Property;

      (7)   take all necessary precautions to prevent broken water pipes due to freezing or other causes;

      (8)   replace any lost or misplaced keys;

      (9)   pay any periodic, preventive, or additional extermination costs desired by Tenant;

      (10) remove any standing water;

      (11) know the location and operation of the main water cut-off valve and all electric breakers and how to switch the valve or breakers off at appropriate times to mitigate any potential damage; and

      (12) promptly notify Landlord, in writing, of all needed repairs.

  B. Yard Maintenance:

      (1) "*Yard*" means all lawns, shrubbery, bushes, flowers, gardens, trees, rock or other landscaping, and other foliage on or encroaching on the Property or on any easement appurtenant to the Property, and does not include common areas maintained by an owners' association.

      (2) "*Maintain the yard*" means to perform activities such as, but not limited to: (a) mowing, fertilizing, and trimming the yard; (b) controlling pests in the yard; and (c) removing debris from the yard.

(TAR-2001) 8-25-09   Tenants:_____, _____, _____, _____ & Landlord or Landlord's Representative:_____, ____   Page 7 of 14

Residential Lease concerning:_____

(3) Unless prohibited by ordinance or other law, Tenant will water the yard at reasonable and appropriate times including but not limited to the following times: _____
_____
_____. Other than watering, the yard will be maintained as follows:

❐ (a) Landlord, at Landlord's expense, will maintain the yard. Tenant will permit Landlord and Landlord's contractors reasonable access to the yard and will remove any pet from the yard at appropriate times.

❐ (b) Tenant, at Tenant's expense, will maintain the yard.

❐ (c) Tenant will maintain in effect a scheduled yard maintenance contract with: ❐ a contractor who regularly provides such service; ❐ _____.

C. Pool/Spa Maintenance: Any pool or spa on the Property will be maintained according to a Pool/Spa Maintenance Addendum.

D. Prohibitions: If Tenant installs any fixtures on the Property, authorized or unauthorized, such as additional smoke detectors, locks, alarm systems, cables, satellite dishes, or other fixtures, such fixtures will become the property of the Landlord. Except as otherwise permitted by law, this lease, or in writing by Landlord, Tenant may not:
(1) remove any part of the Property or any of Landlord's personal property from the Property;
(2) remove, change, add, or rekey any lock;
(3) make holes in the woodwork, floors, or walls, except that a reasonable number of small nails may be used to hang pictures in sheetrock and grooves in paneling;
(4) permit any water furniture on the Property;
(5) install additional phone or video cables, outlets, antennas, satellite receivers, or alarm systems;
(6) replace or remove flooring material, paint, or wallpaper;
(7) install, change, or remove any: fixture, appliance, or non-real-property item listed in Paragraph 2;
(8) keep or permit any hazardous material on the Property such as flammable or explosive materials;
(9) keep or permit any material or item which causes any liability or fire and extended insurance coverage to be suspended or canceled or any premiums to be increased;
(10) dispose of any environmentally detrimental substance (for example, motor oil or radiator fluid) on the Property; or
(11) cause or allow any lien to be filed against any portion of the Property.

E. Failure to Maintain: If Tenant fails to comply with this Paragraph 17 or any Pool/Spa Maintenance Addendum, Landlord may, in addition to exercising Landlord's remedies under Paragraph 27, perform whatever action Tenant is obligated to perform and Tenant must immediately reimburse Landlord the reasonable expenses that Landlord incurs.

18. REPAIRS: (Notice: Subchapter B, Chapter 92, Property Code governs repair obligations).

A. **Repair Requests: All requests for repairs must be in writing and delivered to Landlord. If Tenant is delinquent in rent at the time a repair notice is given, Landlord is not obligated to make the repair. In the event of an emergency related to the condition of the Property that materially affects the physical health or safety of an ordinary tenant, call:_____. Ordinarily, a repair to the heating and air conditioning system is not an emergency.**

B. **Completion of Repairs:**

(1) **Tenant may not repair or cause to be repaired any condition, regardless of the cause, without Landlord's permission. All decisions regarding repairs, including the completion of any repair, whether to repair or replace the item, and the selection of contractors, will be at Landlord's sole discretion.**

Residential Lease concerning:_____

      (2) Landlord is not obligated to complete a repair on a day other than a business day unless required to do so by the Property Code.

C. <u>Payment of Repair Costs</u>: Tenant will pay Landlord or any contractor Landlord directs Tenant to pay, the first $_____ of the cost to repair each condition in need of repair, and Landlord will pay the remainder, except for the following conditions which will be paid as follows.

      (1) <u>Repairs that Landlord will Pay Entirely</u>: Landlord will pay the entire cost to repair:
          (a) a condition caused by the Landlord or the negligence of the Landlord;
          (b) wastewater stoppages or backups caused by deterioration, breakage, roots, ground condition, faulty construction, or malfunctioning equipment;
          (c) a condition that adversely affects the health or safety of an ordinary tenant which is not caused by Tenant, an occupant, a member of Tenant's family, or a guest or invitee of Tenant; and
          (d) a condition in the following items which is not caused by Tenant or Tenant's negligence:
             (1) heating and air conditioning systems;
             (2) water heaters; or
             (3) water penetration from structural defects.

      (2) <u>Repairs that Tenant will Pay Entirely</u>: Tenant will pay Landlord or any contractor Landlord directs Tenant to pay the entire cost to repair:
          (a) a condition caused by Tenant, an occupant, a member of Tenant's family, or a guest or invitee of Tenant (a failure to timely report an item in need of repair or the failure to properly maintain an item may cause damage for which Tenant may be responsible);
          (b) damage from wastewater stoppages caused by foreign or improper objects in lines that exclusively service the Property;
          (c) damage to doors, windows, or screens; and
          (d) damage from windows or doors left open.

      (3) <u>Appliances or Items that will not be Repaired</u>: Landlord does not warrant and will not repair or replace the following:_____
_____.

D. <u>Trip Charges</u>: If a repair person is unable to access the Property after making arrangements with Tenant to complete the repair, Tenant will pay any trip charge the repair person may charge, which amount may be different from the amount stated in Paragraph 14C.

E. <u>Advance Payments and Reimbursements</u>: Landlord may require advance payment of repairs or payments under this Paragraph 18 for which Tenant is responsible. Tenant must promptly reimburse Landlord the amounts under this Paragraph 18 for which Tenant is responsible.

F. <u>NOTICE</u>: If Landlord fails to repair a condition that materially affects the physical health or safety of an ordinary tenant as required by this lease or the Property Code, Tenant may be entitled to exercise remedies under §92.056 and §92.0561 of the Property Code. If Tenant follows the procedures under those sections, the following remedies may be available to Tenant: (1) terminate the lease and obtain an appropriate refund under §92.056(f); (2) have the condition repaired or remedied according to §92.0561; (3) deduct from the rent the cost of the repair or remedy according to §92.0561; and (4) obtain judicial remedies according to §92.0563. Do not exercise these remedies without consulting an attorney or carefully reviewing the procedures under the applicable sections. The Property Code presumes that 7 days is a reasonable period of time for the Landlord to repair a condition unless there are circumstances which establish that a different period of time is appropriate (such as the severity and nature of

(TAR-2001) 8-25-09   Tenants:_____, _____, _____, _____ & Landlord or Landlord's Representative:_____, ____   Page 9 of 14

Residential Lease concerning:_____

the condition and the availability of materials, labor, and utilities. **Failure to strictly follow the procedures in the applicable sections may cause Tenant to be in default of the lease.**

19. **SECURITY DEVICES AND EXTERIOR DOOR LOCKS:**

   A. Subchapter D, Chapter 92, Property Code requires the Property to be equipped with certain types of locks and security devices. Landlord has rekeyed the security devices since the last occupant vacated the Property or will rekey the security devices within 7 days after Tenant moves in. "Security device" has the meaning assigned to that term in §92.151, Property Code.

   B. All notices or requests by Tenant for rekeying, changing, installing, repairing, or replacing security devices must be in writing. Installation of additional security devices or additional rekeying or replacement of security devices desired by Tenant will be paid by Tenant in advance and may be installed only by contractors authorized by Landlord.

20. **SMOKE DETECTORS:** Subchapter F, Chapter 92, Property Code requires the Property to be equipped with smoke detectors in certain locations. Requests for additional installation, inspection, or repair of smoke detectors must be in writing. Disconnecting or intentionally damaging a smoke detector or removing a battery without immediately replacing it with a working battery may subject Tenant to civil penalties and liability for damages and attorney fees under §92.2611, Property Code.

21. **LIABILITY:** Unless caused by Landlord, Landlord is <u>not</u> responsible to Tenant, Tenant's guests, family, or occupants for any damages, injuries, or losses to person or property caused by fire, flood, water leaks, ice, snow, hail, winds, explosion, smoke, interruption of utilities, theft, burglary, robbery, assault, vandalism, other persons, condition of the Property, environmental contaminants (for example, carbon monoxide, asbestos, radon, lead-based paint, mold, fungus, etc.), or other occurrences or casualty losses. Tenant will promptly reimburse Landlord for any loss, property damage, or cost of repairs or service to the Property caused by Tenant, Tenant's guests, any occupants, or any pets.

22. **HOLDOVER:** If Tenant fails to vacate the Property at the time this lease ends Tenant will pay Landlord rent for the holdover period and indemnify Landlord and prospective tenants for damages, including but not limited to lost rent, lodging expenses, costs of eviction, and attorneys' fees. Rent for any holdover period will be three (3) times the monthly rent, calculated on a daily basis, and will be immediately due and payable daily without notice or demand.

23. **RESIDENTIAL LANDLORD'S LIEN:** Landlord will have a lien for unpaid rent against all of Tenant's nonexempt personal property that is in the Property and may seize such nonexempt property if Tenant fails to pay rent. Subchapter C, Chapter 54, Property Code governs the rights and obligations of the parties regarding Landlord's lien. Landlord may collect a charge for packing, removing, or storing property seized in addition to any other amounts Landlord is entitled to receive. Landlord may sell or dispose of any seized property in accordance with the provisions of §54.045, Property Code.

24. **SUBORDINATION:** This lease and Tenant's leasehold interest are and will be subject, subordinate, and inferior to: (i) any lien or encumbrance now or later placed on the Property by Landlord; (ii) all advances made under any such lien or encumbrance; (iii) the interest payable on any such lien or encumbrance; (iv) any and all renewals and extensions of any such lien or encumbrance; (v) any restrictive covenant; and (vi) the rights of any owners' association affecting the Property.

25. **CASUALTY LOSS OR CONDEMNATION:** Section 92.054, Property Code governs the rights and obligations of the parties regarding a casualty loss to the Property. Any proceeds, payment for damages, settlements, awards, or other sums paid because of a casualty loss to the Property will be Landlord's sole property. For the purpose of this lease, any condemnation of all or a part of the Property is a casualty loss.

(TAR-2001) 8-25-09   Tenants:_____, _____, _____, _____ & Landlord or Landlord's Representative:_____, _____   Page 10 of 14

Residential Lease concerning:_____

26. SPECIAL PROVISIONS: *(Do not insert a lease-option or lease-purchase clause without the assistance of legal counsel. Special obligations and liabilities under statute apply to such transactions.)*

27. DEFAULT:

A. If Landlord fails to comply with this lease, Tenant may seek any relief provided by law.

B. If Tenant fails to timely pay all amounts due under this lease or otherwise fails to comply with this lease, Tenant will be in default and:
    (1) Landlord may terminate Tenant's right to occupy the Property by providing Tenant with at least one day written notice to vacate;
    (2) all unpaid rents which are payable during the remainder of this lease or any renewal period will be accelerated without notice or demand;
    (3) Landlord may exercise Landlord's lien under Paragraph 23 and any other rights under this lease or the Property Code; and
    (4) Tenant will be liable for:
        (a) any lost rent;
        (b) Landlord's cost of reletting the Property including but not limited to leasing fees, advertising fees, utility charges, and other fees reasonably necessary to relet the Property;
        (c) repairs to the Property for use beyond normal wear and tear;
        (d) all Landlord's costs associated with eviction of Tenant, including but not limited to attorney's fees, court costs, costs of service, witness fees, and prejudgment interest;
        (e) all Landlord's costs associated with collection of amounts due under this lease, including but not limited to collection fees, late charges, and returned check charges; and
        (f) any other recovery to which Landlord may be entitled by law.

C. Notice to vacate under Paragraph 27B(1) may be by any means permitted by §24.005, Property Code.

D. Landlord will attempt to mitigate any damage or loss caused by Tenant's breach by attempting to relet the Property to acceptable tenants and reducing Tenant's liability accordingly.

28. EARLY TERMINATION: This lease begins on the Commencement Date and ends on the Expiration date unless: (i) renewed under Paragraph 4; (ii) extended by written agreement of the parties; or (iii) terminated earlier under Paragraph 27, by agreement of the parties, applicable law, or this Paragraph 28.

(TAR-2001) 8-25-09   Tenants:_____, _____, _____, _____ & Landlord or Landlord's Representative:_____, ____   Page 11 of 14

Residential Lease concerning:_____

A. <u>Military and Family Violence</u>: Tenants may have special statutory rights to terminate the lease early in certain situations involving family violence or a military deployment or transfer.

    (1) <u>Military</u>: If Tenant is or becomes a servicemember or a dependent of a servicemember, Tenant may terminate this lease by delivering to Landlord a written notice of termination and a copy of an appropriate government document providing evidence of: (a) entrance into military service; (b) military orders for a permanent change of station (PCS); or (c) military orders to deploy with a military unit for not less than 90 days. Termination is effective on the 30th day after the first date on which the next rental payment is due after the date on which the notice is delivered. Section 92.017, Property Code governs the rights and obligations of the parties under this paragraph.

    (2) <u>Family Violence</u>: Tenant may terminate this lease if Tenant obtains and provides Landlord with a copy of a court order described under §92.016, Property Code protecting Tenant or an occupant from family violence committed by a cotenant or occupant of the Property. Section 92.016, Property Code governs the rights and obligations of the parties under this paragraph.

B. <u>Assignment and Subletting</u>:

    (1) Tenant may not assign this lease or sublet the Property without Landlord's written consent.

    (2) If Tenant requests an early termination of this lease under this Paragraph 28B, Tenant may attempt to find a replacement tenant and may request Landlord to do the same. Landlord may, but is not obligated to, attempt to find a replacement tenant under this paragraph.

    (3) Any assignee, subtenant, or replacement tenant must, in Landlord's discretion, be acceptable as a tenant and must sign: (a) a new lease with terms not less favorable to Landlord than this lease or otherwise acceptable to Landlord; (b) a sublease with terms approved by Landlord; or (c) an assignment of this lease in a form approved by Landlord.

    (4) At the time Landlord agrees to permit an assignee, subtenant, or replacement tenant to occupy the Property, Tenant will pay Landlord:

        (a) if Tenant procures the assignee, subtenant, or replacement tenant:
        ❏ (i) $_____.
        ❏ (ii) _____% of one's month rent that the assignee, subtenant, or replacement tenant is to pay.

        (b) if Landlord procures the assignee, subtenant, or replacement tenant:
        ❏ (i) $_____.
        ❏ (ii) _____% of one's month rent that the assignee, subtenant, or replacement tenant is to pay.

    (5) Unless expressly stated otherwise in an assignment or sublease, Tenant will not be released from Tenant's obligations under this lease because of an assignment or sublease. An assignment of this lease or a sublease of this lease without Landlord's written consent is voidable by Landlord.

29. ATTORNEY'S FEES: Any person who is a prevailing party in any legal proceeding brought under or related to the transaction described in this lease is entitled to recover prejudgment interest, attorney's fees, costs of service, and all other costs of the legal proceeding from the non-prevailing party.

30. REPRESENTATIONS: Tenant's statements in this lease and any application for rental are material representations. Each party to this lease represents that he or she is of legal age to enter into a contract. If Tenant makes a misrepresentation in this lease or in an application for rental, Tenant is in default.

31. ADDENDA: Incorporated into this lease are the following addenda, exhibits and other information. If Landlord's Rules and Regulations are made part of this lease, Tenant agrees to comply with the Rules and Regulations as Landlord may, at Landlord's discretion, amend from time to time.

(TAR-2001) 8-25-09   Tenants:_____, _____, _____, _____ & Landlord or Landlord's Representative:_____, _____   Page 12 of 14

Residential Lease concerning:_____

☐ Addendum Regarding Lead-Based Paint	☐ Agreement Between Brokers
☐ Inventory & Condition Form	☐ Landlord's Rules & Regulations
☐ Landlord's Additional Parking Rules	☐ Owners' Association Rules
☐ Pet Agreement	☐ Pool/Spa Maintenance Addendum
☐ Protecting Your Home from Mold	☐ Residential Lease Application
☐ Agreement for Application Deposit & Hold	☐ Residential Lease Guaranty
☐ _____	☐ _____

32. NOTICES: All notices under this lease must be in writing and are effective when hand-delivered, sent by mail, or sent by electronic transmission to *(Do not insert an e-mail address or a fax number unless the party consents to receive notices under this lease at the e-mail address or fax number specified.)*:

Tenant at the Property and a copy to: Landlord c/o:

_____   _____
_____   _____
_____   _____
E-mail:_____   E-mail:_____
Fax: _____   Fax: _____

33. AGREEMENT OF PARTIES:

     A. <u>Entire Agreement</u>: There are no oral agreements between Landlord and Tenant. This lease contains the entire agreement between Landlord and Tenant and may not be changed except by written agreement.

     B. <u>Binding Effect</u>: This lease is binding upon and inures to the benefit of the parties to this lease and their respective heirs, executors, administrators, successors, and permitted assigns.

     C. <u>Joint and Several</u>: All Tenants are jointly and severally liable for all provisions of this lease. Any act or notice to, refund to, or signature of, any one or more of the Tenants regarding any term of this lease, its extension, its renewal, or its termination is binding on all Tenants executing this lease.

     D. <u>Waiver</u>: Landlord's past delay, waiver, or non-enforcement of a rental due date or any other right will not be deemed to be a waiver of any other breach by Tenant or any other right in this lease.

     E. <u>Severable Clauses</u>: Should a court find any clause in this lease unenforceable, the remainder of this lease will not be affected and all other provisions in this lease will remain enforceable.

     F. <u>Controlling Law</u>: The laws of the State of Texas govern the interpretation, validity, performance, and enforcement of this lease.

     G. <u>Copyright</u>: If an active REALTOR® member of the Texas Association of REALTORS® or an active member of the State Bar of Texas does not negotiate this lease as a party or for one of the parties, either as a party's broker or attorney, this lease is voidable at will by Tenant.

34. INFORMATION:

     A. Future inquires about this lease, rental payments, and security deposits should be directed to the person listed for receipt of notices for Landlord under Paragraph 32.

(TAR-2001) 8-25-09   Tenants:_____, _____, _____, _____ & Landlord or Landlord's Representative:_____, ____   Page 13 of 14

Residential Lease concerning:_____

B. It is Tenant's responsibility to determine, before signing this lease, if: (i) all services (e.g., utilities, connections, schools, and transportation) are accessible to or from the Property; (ii) such services are sufficient for Tenant's needs and wishes; and (iii) Tenant is satisfied with the Property's condition.

C. The brokers to this lease have no knowledge of whether Landlord is delinquent in the payment of any lien against the Property.

D. Unpaid rent and any unpaid amount under this lease are reportable to credit reporting agencies.

E. Landlord is not obligated to respond to any requests for Tenant's rental and payment history from a mortgage company or other prospective landlord until Tenant has given notice of termination of this lease and Tenant is not in breach of this lease. (*Notice: Landlord or Landlord's agent may charge a reasonable fee for processing such information.*)

F. If all occupants over 18 years of age die during this lease, Landlord may: (i) permit the person named below to access the Property at reasonable times in Landlord's or Landlord's agent's presence; (ii) permit the named person to remove Tenant's personal property; and (iii) refund the security deposit, less deductions, to the named person. Section 92.014, Property Code governs procedures to follow in the event of a tenant's death.
    Name: _____ Phone: _____
    Address: _____
    E-mail: _____

G. The Texas Department of Public Safety maintains a database that the public may search, at no cost, to determine if registered sex offenders are located in certain areas (see www.txdps.state.tx.us under on-line services). For information concerning past criminal activity in certain areas, contact the local police department.

H. Landlord's insurance does not cover Tenant from loss of personal property. Landlord recommends that Tenant obtain insurance for casualties such as fire, flood, water damage, and theft. Tenant represents that Tenant ❏ intends ❏ does not intend to purchase such insurance.

I. Landlord's broker, _____,
    ❏ will ❏ will not act as the property manager for landlord.

J. This lease is negotiable between the parties. This lease is binding upon final acceptance. READ IT CAREFULLY. If you do not understand the effect of this lease, consult your attorney BEFORE signing.

_____ _____   _____ _____
Landlord   Date   Tenant   Date

_____ _____   _____ _____
Landlord   Date   Tenant   Date

Or signed for Landlord under written property management   _____ _____
agreement or power of attorney: Tenant   Date

By: _____
                             Date   _____ _____
                                           Tenant   Date

Printed Name: _____

Firm Name: _____

(TAR-2001) 8-25-09   Page 14 of 14

The sections contained in the TAR Residential Lease Agreement are found below.

1. Parties

Section 1 requires the broker to fill in the name of the landlord and the name of the tenant because they are the parties to the lease agreement. The names of the parties entered in this section should be accurate and contain the correct spelling.

2. Property

If the lease is for one year or more, Section 2 requires the broker to describe the property using the street address and legal property description. The accuracy of the property information is also important in order to avoid costly mistakes should there be any legal arbitration.

3. Term

Section 4 describes the **term**, which is the length of time for which the lease will run. It is indicated by the commencement date and the termination date. According to this section, the tenant is given five days to occupy the property after the commencement date. However, if the tenant is unable to occupy the property due to construction, or if a previous tenant is still living in the property, the tenant can terminate the lease agreement.

4. Automatic Renewal and Notice of Termination

Section 4 deals with the automatic renewal of the lease or its termination. The lease will renew by default at the end of the lease term and revert to a month-to-month lease unless either party provides the other party with a written notice of termination at least 30 days before the expiration date or the end of the renewal period.

Once the lease has converted to a month-to-month basis, it may be terminated by either party by providing written notice to the other party. In this case, the lease would either terminate on a date specified in the notice as long as it is not sooner than 30 days from the notice date; or the lease would terminate on the last day of the month in which the notice is given if the notice was given on the first day of that month. However, if the notice was given on any other day of that month, the lease will not terminate until the last day of the following month. Any notice to terminate a lease must be in writing under all circumstances. Therefore, an oral agreement is not acceptable.

5. Rent

Section 5 outlines the rent due as part of the lease agreement. The broker fills in the amount of rent due for each full month during the lease, the date on which the rent is due for the first full month, and for each subsequent month thereafter.

The broker must also fill in any prorated rent the tenant must pay, how much, and on what date. The form also asks for the name of the payee and the address or other location where the rent should be submitted each month.

The tenant must pay the rent by check, money order, cashier's check, or some other means deemed acceptable by the landlord. If there are multiple tenants in the property, the landlord has the right to require the total rent be paid by one check.

The landlord is not required to pay user fees for the tenant's use of common areas on the property, such as a pool or tennis courts.

The landlord may not increase the rent on the property before the termination date; however, if the lease is renewed on a month-to-month basis, the landlord may increase the rent provided he or she gives written notice to the tenant at least 30 days in advance.

6. Late Charges

Section 6 addresses late charges and the terms on how are they are assessed. If the tenant fails to pay the rent on time in any month, the tenant must pay the landlord an initial late charge of a specified amount, plus late charges, every day until the rent is paid in full. If the landlord receives the rent by a certain day of the month (to be specified by the landlord), the landlord will waive the late charges. However, even if the tenant pays the rent before the specified date and the landlord does not charge him or her the late fees, the landlord is not prohibited from reporting the tenant to a consumer-reporting agency.

7. Returned Checks

Section 7 addresses returned checks. If the tenant submits a bad check to the landlord, the tenant must pay a fee not to exceed $25.00, as well as initial and additional late charges until the landlord has received full payment.

8. Application of Funds

Section 8 refers to the allocation of funds. The landlord must apply any money he or she receives from the tenant first to any non-rent obligations, such as late charges, returned check charges, charge-backs for repairs,

TEXAS LAW OF CONTRACTS

brokerage fees, and periodic utilities. The remaining money may then be used for rent.

9. Pets

Section 9 addresses pets on the property. Pets are prohibited unless the lease agreement is accompanied by a separate, written agreement authorizing pets. The tenants may not keep a pet, even temporarily, on the property, and if the tenant violates the pet restrictions, a landlord can exercise various options. The tenant must pay the landlord a specified fee per pet for each day the pet remains on the property. The landlord can remove any unauthorized pet with at least 24-hour notice to the tenant and the landlord will not be liable for any harm, injury, death, or sickness to the unauthorized pet. The tenant must also pay for any property damage caused by the unauthorized pet, as well as any costs the landlord incurs in the process of removing the pet. A landlord can choose to take one or all of these measures if a tenant violates this section.

10. Security Deposit

Section 10 addresses the **security deposit** due to the landlord. The security deposit is the initial deposit by a tenant that insures compliance with the lease agreement and compensation to the landlord for property damages. It is frequently equal to one month's rent.

The tenant must pay the specified amount to the landlord who must then place that money in an interest bearing account. The tenant may not attempt to withhold a portion of the last month's rent on grounds that the security deposit is security for unpaid rent. This may subject the tenant to charges of up to three times the rent withheld, as well as the landlord's attorney's fees.

If the lease is terminated and the tenant surrenders the property, the landlord has 30 days to refund the security deposit or account for its withholding from the date of surrender. The landlord may deduct certain charges from the security deposit. If the deductions exceed the amount of the security deposit, the tenant must pay the landlord the difference within 10 days of the landlord's demand. This section lists the different types of deductions the landlord can take from the security deposit.

11. Utilities

Section 11 refers to utilities. The tenant must pay connection, service, and usage fees for all utilities except for those specified by the landlord. The tenant is responsible for keeping certain utilities on during the lease term; failure to do so will result in default by the tenant. Gas, electricity, water wastewater, and garbage services are the minimum utilities that a tenant must maintain unless they are provided by the landlord.

12. Use and Occupancy

Section 12 addresses the use and occupancy of the property. The property must be used only as a private dwelling and if the tenant fails to take possession and occupy the property within 5 days of the commencement date, the tenant will be in default. Blanks are provided in this section to list specific individuals who will reside on the property during the duration of the lease.

If the tenant changes any phone numbers, the landlord must be informed within 5 days. In addition, the tenant must comply with all owners' association rules or covenants governing the property.

A landlord must give a tenant exclusive and actual possession of the premises. Therefore, if the premises are occupied by a holdover tenant at the start of the new tenant's lease, the landlord must do whatever is needed to recover possession from the holdover tenant and transfer it to the new tenant.

The tenant may only use the property in certain ways, and is prohibited from allowing the property to be used in other ways specified on the form. This section also specifies that the tenant cannot install certain items that may affect insurance premiums on the property like pools or spas. The tenant may not allow any guests to reside on the property longer than a specified number of days or the amount of time permitted by the owners' association, whichever is shorter.

13. Parking Rules

Section 13 addresses vehicles. The tenant is restricted in the number of vehicles that may be kept on the property and where the vehicles are parked or stored. If the tenant violates these restrictions, the landlord may tow the vehicle at the tenant's expense.

14. Access by Landlord

Section 14 addresses access to the property. The landlord retains access to the property during the lease term and may enter the property without notice for specified reasons. The landlord also retains the right to post signs on the property during the lease or renewal term. The lease form requires the tenant to either authorize or prohibit the landlord from using a keybox on the property to allow entry to others. If the tenant does authorize a keybox, he or she has the right to rescind the authorization via written notice to the landlord and by paying a fee to the landlord as consideration. If the tenant authorizes the keybox, he or she acknowledges that the landlord and the landlord's broker are not responsible for damage, loss, or injury resulting from the use of the keybox.

15. Move-In Condition

Section 15 does not require any completion; it is a confirmation that the tenant has inspected and accepts the rental property as-is, unless the condition is hazardous to a person's health and/or safety. It also releases the landlord from any liability for the condition of the property. The tenant must complete an inspection of the property and an Inventory and Condition Form within 48 hours after the lease's commencement date. If the tenant fails to complete the form, he or she is assumed to accept the property's condition.

16. Move-Out

Section 16 addresses the move-out condition of the property. Upon termination of the lease, the tenant must leave the property as he or she found it, excepting normal wear and tear. Normal wear and tear refers to reasonable deterioration that is not the result of negligence, carelessness, accident, or abuse. The tenant must also remove all personal property, trash, and debris when surrendering the property. If the tenant leaves any personal property behind, it will be forfeited and become the landlord's property.

17. Property Maintenance

Section 17 describes the property maintenance that is the responsibility of the tenant, as well as that which is the responsibility of the landlord. The tenant is expected to perform certain maintenance on the property, while other maintenance can be performed by either the tenant or landlord. The broker or landlord must indicate on the lease if the tenant is responsible for the yard maintenance and pool or spa maintenance.

The last part of Section 17 deals with any fixtures the tenant may install on or in the property, such as smoke detectors, locks, or alarm systems. If the tenant installs any such fixtures, they become the landlord's property. The tenant is also prohibited from installing specific fixtures, as listed in the lease.

18. Repairs

Section 18 addresses property repairs and who is responsible for the repairs. Any repair request made on the property must be in writing and delivered to the landlord. If the tenant makes a request for a repair, but is delinquent on their rent, the landlord does not have to honor the request. The completion of repairs ultimately requires the landlord's permission regardless of the nature of the repair.

A tenant may be obligated to pay a certain amount of the repair with the landlord covering the remaining balance. Depending on the circumstances, the party responsible for the entire amount of the repairs will vary. The tenant is generally responsible for repairs to damage caused by the tenant themselves, current occupants, or guests. Also, any damage to the plumbing due to a foreign object, and damage to doors, windows, and screens are paid by the tenant.

The landlord is generally responsible for repairs due to damage caused by the landlord's negligence, deterioration, breakage, faulty construction, or tree roots. Also, a landlord is responsible for any repairs that affect the health or safety of a tenant or guest.

The landlord can specify certain items he or she will not be held responsible for in this section. The tenant may be responsible for costs involved if a repair person cannot access the property. Furthermore, if the tenant is responsible for damages, the landlord can elect to receive advance payments for the repairs.

19. Security Devices and Exterior Door Locks

Section 19 refers to security devices and locks. If the tenant needs or wants new keys to the property, or needs or wants to change, install, repair, or replace any security devices for the property, he or she must submit the request to the landlord in writing. The landlord must fulfill the request no later than 7 days after the new tenant moves in. If the tenant installs new locks, he or she must first submit the request to the landlord in writing and give the landlord a key.

20. Smoke Detectors

Section 20 addresses smoke detectors. The property must be equipped with smoke detectors in certain locations according to the Texas Property Code. If the tenant needs or wants additional smoke detectors, inspection, or repair of smoke detectors, he or she must submit the request in writing. The tenant is prohibited from disconnecting or intentionally damaging a smoke detector and may be subject to civil penalties under the Texas Property Code. The tenant is responsible for replacing the batteries as needed.

21. Liability

Section 21 states that the landlord is not responsible for damages, injuries, or loss to the tenant or tenant's family or guests due to a variety of causes, such as flood, fire, theft, and environmental contaminants. In addition, the tenant must reimburse the landlord in the event of property damage or loss caused by the tenant's negligence or improper use of the property.

22. Holdover

Section 22 addresses holdovers. If at the termination of the lease or at the end of the renewal period, the tenant fails to vacate the property, a holdover period begins and the tenant must pay for this period at a rate of two times the monthly rent, calculated on a daily basis. This holdover rent is due daily and without notice. The tenant must also reimburse the landlord and any prospective new tenants for lost rent, lodging expenses, and attorney's fees.

23. Residential Landlord's Lien

Section 23 refers to a residential landlord's lien. If the tenant fails to pay rent, the landlord may place a lien on the tenant's non-exempt personal property that is in the leased property and the landlord may charge the tenant a fee for any packing, removing, and storing of the personal property.

24. Subordination

Section 24 addresses subordination. While the tenant and landlord are held to the provisions of the lease, under certain circumstances other agreements may take precedence. These include liens or encumbrances already on the property, restrictive covenants, and the rights of an owners' association.

25. Casualty Loss or Condemnation

Section 25 addresses casualty loss or condemnation. The Texas Property Code states that any proceeds, payment for damages, settlements, awards, or other money paid as a result of a casualty loss to the property will go to the landlord.

26. Special Provisions

Section 26 is a blank space that may be completed with any special provisions the landlord or tenant would like to add to the lease agreement.

27. Default

Section 27 addresses both parties if either of them fails to comply with the lease agreement. The tenant can seek remedies under law if the landlord defaults on the contract. If the tenant is in default, the landlord can exercise a number of options. The landlord can terminate the tenant's right to occupy the property, demand the full amount of the remaining payments on the lease, place a lien on the tenant's personal property, or exercise other remedies stated in this section.

28. Early Termination

Section 28 addresses the right of the tenant to terminate the lease agreement under special circumstances. If a tenant or dependent of the tenant becomes involved in military service, he or she can terminate the agreement if a written notice and proper documentation is given to the landlord. A tenant can also terminate the lease if he or she can provide court evidence showing family violence by a cotenant of the property.

This section also addresses the rules for assigning or subletting the lease. An **assignment** is the transfer of the entire leasehold estate to a new person, called an **assignee**. The original lessee (**assignor**) steps out of primary responsibility for the lease and a new lessee (assignee) becomes responsible to the landlord for all the terms of the original rental agreement. A **sublease** or **sublet** transfers possession of a leased property to a new person called the **sublessee**. The original tenant, who is now the **sublessor**, is still primarily liable for paying the rent to the owner. The sublessee is liable only to the sublessor. Under the lease agreement, a tenant must obtain written permission from the landlord before assigning or subletting the lease.

29. Attorney's Fees

Section 29 refers to attorney's fees. In the event of a legal proceeding relating to the lease, the non-prevailing party must pay the prevailing party's prejudgment interest, attorney's fees, and any other litigation costs.

30. Representations

Statements made by the tenant under this lease agreement become material representations. By entering into the agreement, each party represents that they are of legal age to contract and if either party makes a misrepresentation, they are in default of the contract.

31. Addenda

Section 31 is a checklist of any addenda that are attached as part of the lease. The addenda include a pet addendum, the Inventory and Condition Form, and a Lead-Based Paint addendum. If any of these addenda apply to the lease agreement, they must be completed and attached to the lease agreement.

32. Notices

Section 32 refers to notices regarding the lease. This section specifies the address where the landlord wishes any notices to be delivered. All notices for the tenant will be delivered to the leased property address. All documents must be written and become effective once hand-delivered, mailed, or faxed.

33. Agreement of Parties

Section 33 lists the main provisions under this lease that both parties willingly agree to.

The landlord and tenant under this section agree that:

- only a written agreement can replace this lease agreement if any items are changed.

- the lease is a binding contract.

- tenants and cotenants are liable for adhering to the lease agreement as individuals and as a group.

- any waiver in rent by the landlord does not give the tenant the right to a waiver in a breach or right in the contract.

- if a court deems the lease agreement unenforceable, the provisions of the lease will remain intact.

- the state of Texas will govern the provisions of the lease.

- the lease is voidable by the tenant if a member of the Texas Association of REALTORS® does not negotiate this lease.

34. Information

The final section of the lease agreement form includes any additional information pertinent to the contract.

Information in Section 34 states that:

- inquiries regarding the lease should be delivered to the addresses provided in Section 32.

- the tenant is ultimately responsible for approving the condition of the property prior to signing the lease.

- brokers involved in this lease agreement are unaware of any liens on the property.

- the person named in the spaces provided has the right to access the property should all persons over the age of 18 become deceased under the lease agreement.

- a database is available under the Texas Department of Public Safety for identifying registered sex offenders within the area.

- insurance provided by the landlord will not cover the tenant's loss of personal property.

- the landlord's broker will or will not act as the property manager.

- the lease agreement is negotiable and becomes a binding agreement once all parties give final acceptance to its provisions.

Summary

A **lease** is a contract in which a property owner offers a proposed tenant the right to occupy the property for a specific amount of time. The property owner leasing the property is the **lessor** or landlord and the tenant is the **lessee**. The lessor maintains a **reversionary right** meaning that the property reverts to the lessor when the lease expires.

The elements in creating a valid lease are similar to that of creating a valid contract. They include legal **competency of parties**, **mutual consent**, **lawful objective**, **consideration**, and a **legal description**. The only difference is that according to the Statute of Frauds, a lease for more than one year must be in writing. Lease agreements with duration of less than one year may be made orally.

The tenant's right to occupy the property under the terms of a lease agreement is the definition of a **leasehold estate**. The different types of leasehold estates are an **estate for years**, a **periodic estate**, a **tenancy at will**, and a **tenancy at sufferance**.

The Statute of Frauds in Texas calls for lease agreements to be in writing if they last for more than one year. However, landlords will typically put a lease agreement in writing even if it is less than one year. A common form of lease agreement in Texas is the **Residential Lease** created by the Texas Association of REALTORS®. Real estate licensees should be familiar with each section of the lease and fill the form out as accurately as possible.

Unit 9

Real Estate Disclosures

Introduction

As the buying and selling of real property becomes more complex, real estate contracts become more complex as well. **Caveat emptor**, a Latin phrase meaning, "**let the buyer beware**", is becoming a thing of the past. No longer is the buyer put on notice to examine the property and buy it at his or her own risk. Now, consumer protection laws place the responsibility for disclosing the condition of the property on the seller and the broker. As a real estate practitioner, you are required to guide all parties through the disclosure process. A purchase agreement can become void or voidable and ruin a deal if proper disclosures are not made. In addition, a licensee or seller may be held liable for failing to make required disclosures. Therefore, when creating a sales contract, it is important to include necessary disclosures to supplement the transaction.

Learning Objectives

After reading this unit, you should be able to:

- define disclosures and understand their necessity.
- identify required disclosures in real estate.
- explain the legal consequences of not disclosing information.
- state specific examples of not disclosing information.

Disclosures Required in Agency Relationships

As you previously learned, brokers work within a legal relationship called an agency. The agency relationship exists between the broker, as agent, and the principal. The essence of the agency relationship is that the agent has the authority to represent the principal. Agents and their sales associates are legally obligated to protect and promote the interests of the principal as they would their own.

Although homebuyers and sellers use the services of real estate agents, most of them have limited understanding of the agency representation. Therefore, real estate agents are required to provide an **agency disclosure**

statement at the first personal meeting with potential sellers or buyers. This statement gives the client the opportunity to find out who will represent them and if there are any conflicts of interest.

Information about Brokerage Services

The promulgated form for the agency disclosure statement is called **Information about Brokerage Services.** It discloses the agency relationship between the agent and the principal. Texas real estate law requires an agent to give this form to sellers, buyers, landlords, and tenants. The form states that the parties involved in a real estate transaction should be aware of whom an agent is representing. The form also discloses the duties of a real estate broker in the following situations.

Broker Represents Owner

In this particular agency relationship, the broker becomes the agent to the owner selling the home. The broker and seller enter into a listing agreement to form this type of agency relationship. The broker becomes the listing agent for the seller who will compensate the broker if he or she produces a "ready, willing, and able" buyer. Further, the form states that a listing agent may assist a buyer, but he or she must put the owner's interests first.

Broker Represents Buyer

The role of a broker in a fiduciary relationship with a buyer is to obtain the best possible price. In this situation the broker is usually the buyer's agent under a buyer representation agreement. While the buyer's agent can assist the seller, his or her duties rest upon the interests of the buyer.

Broker Acts As Intermediary

As you also learned, a broker could act as an intermediary between both parties. However, a broker must obtain consent from both parties in writing to act as an intermediary in a real estate transaction. The broker must also provide duties to both parties equally without being partial to the interest of one party.

The last paragraph in the Information about Brokerage Services form states that a party in a real estate transaction should obtain a written agreement outlining the agency relationship. This written agreement solidifies that the agency relationship has been made known to both the principal and the agent. The written agreement should also state when and how the broker would be compensated. Be sure to obtain a written agreement outlining the terms because the payment of a fee to an agent does not necessarily establish the agency relationship.

Disclosures Required in Real Estate Transfers

One of the most critical responsibilities imposed on real estate licensees is the **duty of full disclosure**. This means that it is your responsibility to comply with the law for each disclosure required. Many of the required disclosures are enumerated in the sales contract, and it is your responsibility to explain each one to your clients and customers.

Real estate agents must be prepared to meet the duties and obligations required by law. If real estate agents do not comply with the law, they may be subject to civil, criminal, and/or Texas Real Estate Commission action and penalties. All over the country, courts and legislatures are continuing to hold real estate agents accountable for their activities. Increasingly, real estate agents must know what and how to disclose—as well as when, where, why, by, and to whom.

The uninformed real estate agent is highly vulnerable to court action in our consumer-oriented society. For example, in one court action, the buyer proved that the listing agents were negligent because one of the agents had noticed that netting had been placed on a slope to keep the slope in place, and another agent had noticed an uneven floor inside the home—both were the results of an undisclosed soil problem. The court stated that the "red flags" should have indicated to the real estate agents that there was a problem, and the problem should have been investigated. A **red flag** is something that alerts a reasonably observant person to a potential problem. Typically, a red flag could include cracks in walls, foundations, or sidewalks, stains from leaks in the roof, and similar things.

In addition, no property may be sold "as is" without a complete disclosure of the defect, even though a broker might possess a disclaimer of liability for the defect. An **"as is" clause** in a purchase agreement does not relieve a seller from the responsibility to disclose all known material facts to the buyer. However, an "as is" clause indicates that the seller will not be responsible for the cost of repairing any defect. Real estate licensees should continue to encourage sellers to disclose any known defects in the property.

Seller's Disclosure of Property Condition

Texas requires sellers of residential property to provide a **Seller's Disclosure of Property Condition** to any buyer. This notice is a detailed statement that explains what the seller knows about the condition of the property. The statement must list all known defects as well as any potential problems that might affect the property's value. Usually a broker obtains this statement at the time the listing is taken and provides a copy to a buyer before an offer to purchase the property is presented.

The seller reveals any information that would be important to the buyer regarding the condition of the property, and states that—to the seller's knowledge—everything important has been disclosed. Many facts about a residential property could materially affect its value and desirability, including:

- age, condition and any defects or malfunctions of the structural components and/or plumbing, electrical, heating or other mechanical systems.

- room additions, structural alterations, repairs, replacements, or other changes, especially those made without required building permits.

- flooding, drainage, or soil problems on, near, or in any way affecting the property.

- zoning violations, such as nonconforming uses or insufficient setbacks.

- homeowners' association obligations and deed restrictions or common area problems.

- citations against the property or lawsuits against the owner or affecting the property.

- location of the property within a known floodplain.

- any written inspection reports within the last 4 years from individuals who regularly provide inspections on the property.

Completion of Notice

Brokers should encourage the seller to complete this notice without any broker assistance. While brokers are not allowed to help the seller fill out this form, they can help clarify certain items if they appear unclear. Some of the aforementioned disclosures are required to complete the sale of real property, such as the addenda forms previously covered. If the broker assists with an erroneous, incomplete, or false notice, he or she may be held liable.

When Notice Is Not Required

As a broker, you should be knowledgeable about situations where the sellers may be exempt from providing the notice, such as transfers:

- pursuant to a court order.

- by a trustee in bankruptcy.

- to a mortgagor or successor in interest.

- by a mortgagor or beneficiary under a deed of trust who has acquired the real property by way of a court-ordered foreclosure or deed in lieu of foreclosure.

- by a fiduciary in the course of administering an estate, guardianship, conservatorship, or trust.

- from one co-owner to another.

- from one spouse to another.

- from one spouse to another as a result of divorce or legal separation.
- to or from any government entity.
- of new one-unit residences.
- of real property where the improvements do not exceed 5% of the property value as a whole.

Date of Disclosure

The required disclosure must be delivered by the seller no later than the date of the executory contract. Should any disclosure or amended disclosure be delivered after the required date, the buyer/transferee may terminate the offer or agreement to purchase. A written notice of termination must reach the seller/transferor or the seller's agent.

Expert Reports and Opinions

If the buyer receives a report or an opinion prepared by a licensed engineer, land surveyor, geologist, structural pest control operator, contractor, or other expert (with a specific professional license or expertise), the liability of the seller and the real estate agents may be limited when making required disclosures.

Effect of Violation of Disclosure Law

Your overall intention is to provide meaningful disclosures about the condition of the property being transferred. A violation of the law does not invalidate a transfer; however, the seller may be liable for any actual damages suffered by the buyer.

Specific Disclosures Included with Seller's Disclosure Notice

Lead-Based Paint Hazards

The Residential Lead-Based Paint Hazard Reduction Act of 1992 (Title X) became effective on September 6, 1996 for owners of property with four or fewer units. A lead-hazard information brochure and disclosure form must be provided to a buyer or lessee by a seller or landlord. In addition, the presence of any known lead-based paint must be disclosed.

This disclosure pertains to residential housing built before 1978 because the Act banned lead-based paint for residential use in that year. Some pre-1978 properties, called **target housing**, are exempt from the disclosure. They include housing for the elderly and vacation housing.

The seller, landlord, and real estate agent involved in the sale or rental of pre-1978 housing each have certain obligations under the law.

Toxic Mold

Mold is everywhere—in the air and on many surfaces. **Mold** is a fungus that reproduces by means of spores. Molds alone are not toxic or poisonous. However, certain molds are toxigenic because they can produce toxins, called mycotoxins. The Texas Association of REALTORS® recently added mold to its list of environmental hazards on the Seller's Disclosure Notice. Mold assessment involves inspection of the property to evaluate mold presence and extent. Remediation protocol must be followed and a post assessment is required. The contractor will give the property owner a Certificate of Mold Remediation no more than ten days after a mold remediation has passed a clearance inspection. All certificates issued during the previous five years must be furnished to the buyer when the property owner sells the property.

Special Flood Hazard Area (Any Type Zone "A" or "V")

Flood hazard boundary maps identify the general flood hazards within a community, are used in flood plain management, and for flood insurance purposes. These maps, developed by the **Federal Emergency Management Agency (FEMA)** in conjunction with communities participating in the National Flood Insurance Program (NFIP), show areas within a **100-year flood** boundary, termed "special flood zone areas". Also identified are areas between 100 and 500-year levels termed "areas of moderate flood hazards" and the remaining areas above the 500-year level termed "areas of minimal risk".

A seller of property located in a special flood hazard area, or the seller's agent and/or any agent cooperating in the deal, must disclose to the buyer that federal law requires flood insurance as a condition of obtaining financing on most structures located in a special flood hazard area. Since the cost and extent of flood insurance coverage may vary, the buyer should contact an insurance carrier or the intended lender for additional information.

Areas of Potential Flooding

Areas designated on an inundation map may flood as the result of a dam failure. If the property is on a list of properties posted at the County Public Works/Engineering Offices, Assessors Office, Water Agencies, or Planning Agency, the seller or listing broker must disclose this information to a buyer. If the owner has received federal flood disaster assistance, the seller must tell the buyer to purchase flood insurance.

Mandatory Owner's Subdivision Membership

A seller of a property located within a subdivision that requires mandatory membership in a homeowners' association must disclose this by providing a resale certificate called Subdivision Information, including a Resale

Certificate for Property Subject to Mandatory Membership in an Owners' Association.

Additional Statutory Disclosures

Most disclosures required for standard residential properties are already included on the Seller's Disclosure Notice. The following additional disclosures apply only to specific property types like non-residential land or coastal regions.

Rollback Taxes

Qualifying owners of agricultural and other open-space land are entitled to certain tax breaks. The rollback tax disclosure states that when the land use changes to a non-agricultural use, the taxes will be rolled back five years, or three years for ecological laboratories, timberlands, and open agricultural land. The rollback is calculated based on which taxes were paid versus the taxes that should have been paid had the open space benefit not existed. These rollback taxes should specify in the sales contract as to whether the seller or buyer is responsible for paying them.

MUD Forms

A **Municipal Utility District** (MUD) is a government entity located within a city or city's jurisdiction to provide utilities that are otherwise not provided by the city. A MUD may adopt and enforce all necessary charges, fees, and taxes in order to provide district facilities and service. A buyer must be notified if the property of interest is subject to the higher taxes and other fees that result from its inclusion in a MUD.

Two notices are required. The first is provided by the seller or seller's agent at the time of signing the binding sales contract. The second notice is given at closing. The final notice must be signed and acknowledged by the purchaser and recorded with the deed.

Annexation

The seller of property located in the jurisdiction of a city, but outside of the city's boundaries, must provide the buyer with a written notice that the property may be subject to annexation by the local city, now or in the future.

Public Beaches

Texas is an open beach state, meaning that all beaches are public, state-protected easements, and property with a border abutting the beach may have its dimensions legally changed as the vegetation line changes. Sellers of this type of property must include the Addendum for Property Located Seaward of the Gulf Intracoastal Waterway form.

Other Coastal Properties

Sellers of coastal properties that share a boundary with "tidally influenced submerged lands" must include the Addendum for Coastal Area Property to the buyer. This notice states that the property boundary may gain or lose parts of land. It also affirms that only a qualified professional can accurately determine the boundary.

Pipelines

When selling unimproved land for division into residential lots, the seller must disclose if there are any transportation pipelines on or under the property. Transportation pipelines include lines for natural gas, synthetic gas, petroleum gas, or other hazardous products.

Furnishing Controlling Documents

The owner (other than a subdivider) of a separate legal share in a common interest development (community apartment project, condominium project, planned development, or stock cooperative) must provide a prospective buyer with the following:

- A copy of the governing documents of the development.

- Should there be an age restriction not consistent with the law, a statement that the age restriction is only enforceable to the extent permitted by law, and applicable provisions of the law.

- A copy of the homeowners' association's most recent financial statement.

- A written statement from the association specifying the amount of current regular and special assessments as well as any unpaid assessment, late charges, interest and costs of collection which are or may become a lien against the property.

- Any information on any approved change in the assessments or fees not yet due and payable as of the disclosure date.

- A preliminary list of construction defects if the association has commenced or plans to commence an action for damages against the developer.

- After resolution, by settlement agreement or otherwise, of a dispute between the association and developer regarding construction defects, a general description of the defects that will be corrected; the association's estimate of when the corrections will be completed; the status of any claims for other defects.

Stigmatized Property

Real estate agents must be very careful when making disclosures about stigmatized properties. A **stigmatized property**, as defined by the National

Association of REALTORS®, is "a property that has been psychologically impacted by an event which occurred, or was suspected to have occurred, on the property, such event being one that has no physical impact of any kind." Although some might call a haunted house "stigmatized" the most common properties associated with stigmatized property are those in which there have been murders, suicides, or criminal activity.

Neither the transferor (seller/lessor) nor the agent must disclose a death on the property unless the death was caused by natural causes, suicide or by an accident unrelated to the condition of the property. This is specified in the Seller's Disclosure of Property Condition under Section 5.

Additionally, if the seller of the house is diagnosed with AIDS or HIV, the seller is not legally obligated to disclose this material fact. Individuals with AIDS are considered disabled by law and are therefore protected by the fair housing laws. It is illegal for brokers and agents to make unsolicited disclosures concerning whether sellers or property occupants have tested positive for HIV or have been diagnosed with AIDS.

Interstate Land Sales Full Disclosure Act

This federal law regulates land sales where two or more states are involved. Subdividers must conform to this law if they have 50 or more lots in one state and want to sell them in another state. A public report from the U.S. Department of Housing and Urban Development (HUD) must be given to each buyer as a protection from less-than-truthful advertising in far-away places.

Disclosures in Financing

One of the purposes of financing disclosures is to help consumers become better shoppers for loan and settlement services. The required disclosures are given to borrowers during various stages of the transaction. Some disclosures spell out the costs associated with the loan or the settlement; others outline lender servicing, escrow account practices, and describe business relationships between settlement service providers. Examples of different types of disclosures in real estate financing are as follows.

Truth in Lending Act (Reg Z) Disclosures

The Truth in Lending Act requires lenders to disclose the important terms and costs of their loans, including the annual percentage rate (APR), finance charge, the payment terms, and information about any variable-rate feature. The **annual percentage rate (APR)** is the relative cost of credit expressed as a yearly rate. It is the relationship of the total finance charge to the total amount financed, expressed as a percentage. The **finance charge** is the dollar amount the credit will cost. The finance charge does not include appraisal fees or credit report fees. It is composed of any direct or indirect charge as a condition of obtaining credit, including interest, loan fees, finder fees, insurance fees, and mortgage insurance fees (PMI or MMI).

Real Estate Settlement Procedures Act Disclosures

The **Real Estate Settlement Procedures Act** (RESPA) applies to all federally related, one to four unit residential mortgage loans. Lenders must give special disclosures and use special procedures and forms for closing costs on most home loans.

Lenders must furnish a copy of a **Special Information Booklet**, together with a **Good Faith Estimate (GFE)** of the amount or **range** of closing costs to every person from whom the lender receives a written application for any federally related loan. They must be given within three business days or at the time of application. The Good Faith Estimate provides detailed information on escrow costs so that the borrower can shop around for escrow services. Additionally, buyers and borrowers will be able to make informed decisions during the loan/sale transaction and the settlement/escrow process.

Equal Credit Opportunity Act

In order to finance the purchase of real estate, credit is the primary source of third party financing. As a result, the **Equal Credit Opportunity Act** (ECOA) makes sure that all consumers are given an equal chance to obtain credit. This prevents unscrupulous lenders from denying credit to individuals due to discrimination. They may not discriminate on the basis of race, color, religion, sex, national origin, marital status, age (provided the applicant is at least 18) or dependence on public assistance.

Other Disclosures

Staying informed is probably the most important task for real estate agents. Those who make continuing efforts to learn and stay current on the real estate industry will compete successfully in the future. Two excellent sources of current information are the Texas Real Estate Commission (www.trec.state.tx.us) and for members, the Texas Association of REALTORS® (www.tar.org).

Pest Control Inspection and Certification Reports

The law does not require that a structural pest control inspection be performed on real property prior to transfer. Should an inspection report and certification be required as a condition of transfer or obtaining financing, however, it must be done as soon as possible. Before transfer of title or before executing a real property sales contract, the selling agent must deliver to the buyer a copy of the report. There must also be written certification attesting to the presence or absence of wood-destroying termites in the visible and accessible areas of the property. Such an inspection report and written certification must be prepared and issued by a registered structural pest control company.

Upon request from the party ordering such a report, the company issuing the same must divide it into two categories: one to identify the portions of the property where existing damage, infection, or infestation are noted; and the other to point out areas that may have impending damage, infection, or infestation. Lenders usually require that any infestation or damage discovered in part one of the report be corrected prior to close of escrow. The cost of correction is usually paid for by the seller. Since part two of the inspection report does not show actual infestation—just a potential problem, the seller is not obligated to correct it.

Generally, if there is more than one real estate agent in the transaction, the agent who obtained the offer is usually responsible for delivering the report. Delivery of the required documents may be in person or by mail to the buyer. The real estate agent responsible for delivery must retain for three years a complete record of the actions taken to effect delivery. Anyone can get a copy of the pest control report by requesting it from the Structural Pest Control Board and paying a fee.

Foreign Investment in Real Property Tax Act (FIRPTA)

Both federal and state tax laws are affected by the Foreign Investment in Real Property Tax Act (FIRPTA). In both cases, the buyer is responsible for making sure either the proper disclosures have been made and/or the proper funds have been set aside. Generally, the broker and escrow agent will make sure this is done. All documents must be kept by the broker and the buyer for five years.

Federal FIRPTA Disclosure

Federal law requires that a buyer of real property must withhold and send to the Internal Revenue Service (IRS) 10% of the gross sales price if the seller of the real property is a foreign person.

Exceptions

The following exceptions are from the FIRPTA withholding requirement:

- The buyer must sign a Buyer's Affidavit of Residency, stating whether he or she is a resident or citizen, that the sales price of the property does not exceed $300,000, and that the property will be used as a residence.

- The seller, under penalty of perjury, must sign a Seller's Affidavit of Non-Foreign Status, stating that he or she is not a foreigner.

- The seller gives the buyer a qualifying statement obtained through the IRS saying arrangements have been made for the collection of or exemption from the tax.

Due to the number of exceptions and other requirements relating to this law, it is recommended that the IRS be consulted. Sellers, buyers, and the real estate agents involved who desire further advice should consult an attorney, CPA, or other qualified tax advisor.

Home Inspection Notice

A borrower who wants a FHA loan for any residential property of one to four units must receive and sign the notice called "The Importance of a Home Inspection".

Notice Regarding the Advisability of Title Insurance

In an escrow for a sale (or exchange) of real property where no title insurance is to be issued, the buyer (or both parties to an exchange) must be advised in writing to obtain title insurance or to have the abstract examined. The real estate agent conducting this escrow also would be responsible for delivering the notice.

Commissions

The commission fees are stated in the listing agreement and buyer representation agreement under Broker's Fee. All commissions must be in writing and must include the seller's signed promise to pay the commission on the listing agreement.

A broker can share his or her commission with his or her buyer or seller as long as notice is given to the principal (buyer or seller) that he or she is paying this commission or receiving a rebate.

If a broker or broker's agent fails to disclose any commissions, rebates, or direct profit received, they could potentially lose their license.

Summary

One of the most important duties a real estate licensee must fulfill is the **duty of full disclosure**. Full disclosure includes property defects, environmental hazards, ordinances, and special taxes. Real estate agents are legally required to explain disclosures to their clients and customers. If the real estate agent does not comply with Texas disclosure law, they become vulnerable to court action.

The real estate agent is responsible for ensuring that the seller completes, as accurately as possible, the **Seller's Disclosure Notice**, which covers all visual and known defects found on the property. The buyer is to receive the copy of the notice before making the offer to purchase the property. If the buyer receives the copy of the notice after making the offer to purchase the property, the buyer has the option of terminating the contract.

The list of real estate disclosures is long and detailed. Included in this list are **lead-based paint hazards**, **toxic mold**, **areas of potential flooding**, and **association financial statements**. Additional disclosure information includes real estate commissions, real estate taxes, and land sales.

A real estate licensee must remain current on all Texas and federal disclosures or risk court action.

Unit 10

Closing and Escrow Contracts

Introduction

In earlier units, you learned about ownership interests in real estate and the contracts used to transfer the interests. In this unit, the processes to transfer ownership and the contracts or forms involved in a typical closing are explained.

Closing the real estate transaction is the final step on the path that began with a listing agreement. **Closing** is a term that describes the completion of a property transaction. In different areas of the country, it may be called settlement, settlement and transfer, closing title, or closing escrow. **Escrow** is a closing method that uses a neutral third party (an escrow officer) to coordinate the closing. During escrow, instructions are given to both parties to the sales transaction. Each party takes the necessary steps to finalize the transaction, which includes gathering appropriate forms and contracts. This unit introduces the contracts used in the closing of a real estate sales transaction.

Learning Objectives

After reading this unit, you should be able to:

- identify closing documents and costs.
- discuss the contracts involved in real estate financing.
- identify the requirements for a valid escrow arrangement.
- describe the documentation involved in the escrow closing process.

Closing Documents and Costs

In order to complete a successful closing, the seller and buyer have to supply specific information, documents, forms, and contracts.

Closing Documents

To prepare for the closing, paperwork must be gathered and prepared in order to answer questions regarding the status of the property and ensure a smooth transfer of ownership. Sellers and buyers should always keep copies of any documents and security instruments they sign, deliver to, or receive from any party in the real estate transaction.

The Seller's Responsibility

Depending on the agreement between the parties, the seller must provide certain documents at closing.

What Must the Seller Provide?

- Deed or title insurance policy showing legal title and a legal description.
- A current mortgage statement that contains the lender's information and account number. If the seller's loan is to be paid off at close, a request for "Demand for Pay-off" will be sent to the lender. If the loan is to be assumed by the buyer, a request for "Beneficiary Statement" will be sent to the lender.
- Any statements or bills to be prorated at close, such as property taxes.
- Pest Inspection Certificate and proof that any required repair work was completed satisfactorily.
- If required, certificates stating the condition of the roof, water, and sewer or septic systems.
- Homeowners' Association information if the property contains common use areas.
- Relevant documentation, such as copies of lease agreements if the sale involves income property.

The Buyer's Responsibility

The buyer is also responsible for providing necessary documents for closing the transaction. In addition, the buyer must review and approve disclosures relating to the property.

What Must the Buyer Provide?

- Deposited funds and any borrowed funds used to pay the purchase price with the escrow holder
- An arrangement for any borrowed funds to be delivered to the escrow holder
- Deposited funds sufficient for escrow and closing costs
- Homeowners' Fire and Hazard Insurance Policy
- Flood Insurance Policy - lenders may request this for properties located on flood plains

What Should the Buyer Review and Approve?

- Any items to be prorated in escrow
- The terms of any mortgages or deeds of trust to be assumed by the buyer or that will remain an encumbrance on the property
- All new loan documents prior to signing
- The commitment for title insurance for the property (verify there are no items of record affecting the property which have not already been approved by the buyer)
- Any restrictions affecting the property, whether of record or not
- The structural pest control and other reports to be delivered through escrow
- A survey, if requested in the contract or required by the lender

Real Estate Financing

The closing also involves the transfer of funds to finance the real estate transaction. Real estate finance contracts usually involve the borrower of a loan promising to pay back what he or she owes the lender. When a loan is made, the borrower signs a promissory note (or note) that states a certain amount of money has been borrowed. The **promissory note**, then, is the evidence of the debt.

When money is loaned for financing real property, a type of **collateral**, or security, is usually required of the borrower as well as the promise to repay the loan. That means the lender wants some concrete assurance of getting the money back beyond the borrower's written promise to pay. The property being bought or borrowed against is used as the security, or collateral, for the debt. The lender is then more secure about making the loan if assured of the property ownership in case of default, or nonpayment, of the loan.

A promissory note is:

- an unconditional written promise to pay a certain sum of money.
- made by one person to another, both able to legally enter into a contract.
- signed by the maker or borrower.
- payable on demand or at a definite time.
- paid to bearer or to order.
- voluntarily delivered by the borrower and accepted by the lender.

In addition to showing the amount borrowed, a promissory note sets the terms of the loan, such as the interest rate, the repayment plan, and an acceleration clause in the event of default. With that information, you can calculate the payments using a financial calculator, printed amortization schedule, or software.

Security Instruments

The rights and duties of lenders and borrowers are described in a document called a security instrument. **Security instruments** are used to secure promissory notes. The claim a creditor (lender) has in the property of a debtor (borrower) is called a security interest. A **security interest** allows certain assets of a borrower to be set aside so that a creditor can sell them if the borrower defaults on the loan. Proceeds from the sale of those assets may be taken to pay off the debt. In Texas, a deed of trust is the principal instrument used to secure loans on real property.

Deed of Trust

In real estate finance, a **deed of trust** is a security instrument that conveys title of real property from a trustor to a trustee to hold as security for the beneficiary for payment of a debt. The three parties to a deed of trust are the borrower (**trustor**), lender (**beneficiary**), and a neutral third party called a **trustee**.

The trustor (borrower) signs the promissory note and the deed of trust and gives them to the beneficiary (lender) who holds them for the term of the loan. Under the deed of trust, the trustor has **equitable title** and the trustee has "bare" or "naked" legal title to the property.

Although bare legal title is conveyed using a deed of trust it, does not actually convey possession. Possession and equitable title remain with the borrower. **Equitable title (deed of trust)** is the interest held by the trustor under a deed of trust and gives the borrower the equitable right to obtain absolute ownership to the property when legal title is held by the trustee.

Review - Interests Held Under Equitable Title
- Trustor under a deed of trust
- Vendee under a contract for deed
- Buyer of real property from the time the sales contract is signed and earnest money is paid until the closing.

The trustee who has bare legal title acts as an agent for the beneficiary and has only two obligations. The first is to foreclose on the property if there is a default on the loan, and the second is to reconvey the title to the borrower when the debt is repaid in full. When the debt is repaid in full, the beneficiary signs a **Request for Full Reconveyance** and sends it to the trustee requesting the trustee to reconvey title to the borrower. The trustee signs and records a **Deed of Reconveyance** to show the debt has been repaid and to clear the lien from the property. The deed of trust is recorded at the close of escrow. A **fictitious deed of trust** is a recorded deed of trust containing details that apply to later loan documents.

Closing Costs

Closing costs are expenses that must be paid at closing in order to complete a real estate transaction. These costs do not include the cost of the property.

In Texas, the buyer and seller usually negotiate the allocation of these costs. A particular cost may be paid in full by either the buyer or the seller, split evenly, negotiated between the two parties, or prorated.

Paragraph 12 of the commonly used One to Four Family Residential Contract (Resale), TREC 20-8, specifies which parties will pay the various closing costs.

Examples of Closing Costs

- **Property taxes** – money owed to the local or state government for services used by the homeowner. Property taxes are often prorated.
- **Transfer tax** – money paid to state governments to transfer the ownership of property from one owner to another. Transfer tax allows the government to assess property values. This tax may also be known as **documentary tax** or **conveyance tax**. In Texas, documentary transfer taxes do not apply during the closing.
- **Recording fee** – money paid to government agencies, typically county, to legally record documents that concern the property—often paid for by the buyer.
- **Title insurance** – insurance taken out to protect the policyholder against loss due to a problem in the chain of title. Typically, both the owner and lender take out separate policies. Often, the owner pays for his or her policy and the buyer pays for the lender's policy.

Escrow

Escrow involves the authorization of a neutral third party for preparing and gathering the paperwork and coordinating the funding necessary to complete the real estate transaction. It is a small and short-lived trust during which time the paperwork required for the sale of real property is processed.

After escrow is opened, it is the escrow holder's responsibility to follow the instructions of the buyer and seller, and request all parties involved to observe the terms and conditions of the contract. The **escrow holder** (escrow company) does not make decisions for the principals, but acts as a neutral agent of both the buyer and seller. The escrow holder's duty is to follow the directions of the principals to collect and distribute documents and money as agreed upon in the purchase agreement. Escrow coordinates communication between the principals, the agents involved, and any other professionals—such as the lender, title company, or pest control company—whose services are called for in the escrow instructions.

The Escrow Agent

The escrow agent must be a disinterested third party. The selection of the agent may be negotiated by the buyer and seller. In practice, buyers and sellers often rely on their agents to select an escrow agent due to their lack of real estate experience.

Escrow services are offered by a number of businesses. Businesses that specialize in escrow are known as independent escrow companies. Lending institutions, title companies, some attorney's offices, and some real estate brokerages offer escrow services. Many states require escrow agents to be licensed and bonded because they handle important legal documents and large amounts of money.

Basic Requirements for a Valid Escrow

An escrow is opened when a real estate agent brings the signed purchase agreement to the escrow holder, who makes a copy and accepts the document by signing off in the required box. The escrow holder should be concerned that the contract is complete, fully signed, and initialed before accepting it. The contract must be valid before becoming instructions for the escrow.

Every sale escrow has two basic requirements to be valid: a binding contract between the buyer and seller and conditional delivery of transfer documents to a third party.

Binding Contract

The binding contract can be an offer to purchase, sales contract, exchange agreement, option, or mutual escrow instructions of the buyer and seller. The preparation of the contract of sale is important to the escrow phase and cannot be underestimated because many of the instructions written into the contract of sale are later used by the escrow agent as the escrow instructions.

The instructions the escrow agent looks for include: how the escrow agent will receive and hold the purchase price, the conditions that could cause the escrow to terminate, how to distribute the funds to pay closing costs, proration, prior liens, commissions, and more. Therefore, even though the preparation of the contract of sale is done far before the escrow phase starts, the instructions included in it must be written in a clear and concise manner that anticipates their use in escrow. Once the contract of sale is agreed to by the seller and buyer and is signed, neither the seller, nor the buyer, nor any real estate agent involved in the transaction can change its contents.

After the contract of sale is signed, the escrow agent is selected. Some states allow the selection of an escrow agent to be negotiated; others cite which party chooses the agent.

Conditional Delivery

A conditional delivery of transfer documents is the second requirement for a valid escrow. This means that the seller will deliver a signed deed to the buyer. A **deed** is a document that serves as the evidence of conveying title from a grantor to a grantee. In a sales transaction, the seller of the property is the **grantor** and the buyer is the **grantee**. Most Texas real estate transactions use a **general warranty deed**, which is a deed that transfers title and warrants against situations that may affect title to the property.

Sometime before the escrow closes, the seller is asked to sign a deed conveying title to the buyer. Because the seller signs over the ownership to the buyer before getting the money, the escrow holder is instructed to hold the signed deed until funds from the buyer are deposited in escrow. Once all terms of the escrow have been met, conditional delivery of the grant deed has been made.

General Escrow Principles and Rules

Once escrow instructions, or the purchase agreement as escrow instructions, have been signed by the buyer and seller and returned to the escrow holder, neither party may unilaterally change the escrow instructions. Any changes must be made by mutual agreement between the buyer and seller.

Escrow agents do not negotiate the transaction, provide legal or tax advice, or look for defects in the supplied documents. The escrow agent does not have the authority to make changes in the contract upon the direction of the buyer or seller, unless both agree to the change in the form of an amendment or addendum to the purchase agreement.

The broker also has no authority whatsoever to amend or change any part of the escrow instructions without the knowledge of the principals. The written consent of both buyer and seller, in the form of an amendment to the original instructions or an addendum to the purchase agreement, must be given before any change may be made.

As agent for both parties to an escrow, the escrow agent is placed in a position of trust.

Escrow Procedures

In Texas, title companies generally handle closings through escrow. Escrow procedures remain primarily uniform throughout the state. The following procedures typically occur during a real estate closing in Texas.

Open Escrow

The selling agent is the person who usually opens escrow if a real estate agent is involved. That agent often has an earnest money check that must be deposited into escrow or some other trust account no more than three business days after the buyer and seller sign the deposit receipt.

If there is no real estate agent involved, the principals may go ask the escrow officer to prepare instructions according to their agreement.

Prepare Escrow Instructions

Escrow is officially opened when the escrow holder accepts the purchase agreement, signed by all parties to the escrow. Based on the contract of sale, the escrow agent creates the escrow instructions. These instructions must be approved and signed by both the seller and the buyer. When escrow instructions are drawn, the escrow holder prepares them on a computer-generated form, with details of the particular transaction completed in the blank spaces on the form.

Information Typically Found in Escrow Instructions

- Purchase price of the property
- How the buyer will purchase the property (terms)
- How title to the property will be taken (vesting)
- Matters of record about the property (such as an easement)
- Closing date
- Inspections that take place before the close of escrow
- Proration of expenses
- Date of possession
- Documents the escrow agent must prepare (typically deeds)
- Disbursements of funds to cover expenses and closing costs

Order Title Search

When the buyer and seller reach an agreement about the sale of the property, they also select a title company. One of the responsibilities of the escrow officer, after escrow has been opened, is to order a search of the title of the subject property. The title company searches the records for any encumbrances or liens against the property, checks to make sure the seller is the owner of record, and inspects the history of ownership, or chain of title. The purpose is to ensure all transfers of ownership have been recorded correctly, that there are no unexplained gaps and that there are no liens or encumbrances which will not be released. After completing this search, the title company prepares a preliminary title report.

Request Demands and/or Beneficiary Statements

The escrow officer must also ensure that existing loans are paid off, or assumed, depending on the agreement of the buyer and seller. If the existing loan, or the seller's debt, is to be paid off with proceeds from the sale, a demand from the lender holding the note and trust deed is needed, along with the unpaid principal balance and any other amounts that are due. The escrow officer requests a **demand for payoff** of a loan from the lender who holds a loan against the subject property. The exact amount of loans to be paid off must be known so the escrow officer's accounting will be correct at the close of escrow.

If an existing loan is to be assumed, or taken "subject to", a beneficiary statement is requested by the escrow holder from the lender. A **beneficiary statement** is a statement of the unpaid condition of a loan and describes the condition of the debt.

Accept Reports

The parties to an escrow may request any number of reports about the condition of the property. The escrow holder is asked in the instructions to accept any reports submitted into escrow. These may include a structural pest control report (termite report), property inspection report, soil condition report, or environmental report. Any approval from the buyer or seller about a report is held in escrow until needed or given to the appropriate party at the close of escrow.

New Loan Instructions and Documents

Escrow accepts loan documents or instructions about financing the subject property and completes them as directed. The escrow agent gets the buyer's approval of and signature on loan documents and receives and disburses loan funds as instructed.

Fire Insurance Policies

The parties to an escrow agree on fire insurance policies and instruct the escrow officer accordingly. The escrow holder accepts, holds, and delivers any policies and then follows instructions regarding transfer. A lender requires fire insurance and expects the escrow holder and the buyer to be accountable for either a new policy or the transfer of an existing one.

Settlement

The escrow holder is instructed by the buyer and seller about proration and other accounting completed at the close of escrow. **Proration** is the adjustment of interest, taxes, insurance, etc., on a pro-rata basis as of the closing or agreed-upon date. Hazard insurance policies that are terminated prior to the expiration date at the request of the insured are subject to a short rate cancellation fee. A **short rate cancellation fee** is a fee (or penalty) charged to the person who cancels the insurance policy before it expires. The money returned is the unused premium minus administrative expenses. However, if the insurance company cancels the policy early, there is no penalty.

The escrow holder prepares a settlement (closing) statement for all parties to the escrow. A **settlement statement** is a complete breakdown of all cash received, all charges and credits made, and all costs involved in the transaction. The most common settlement statement used in Texas is the **HUD-1 Settlement Statement** from the U.S. Department of Housing and Urban Development. The statement shows how all closing costs and prepaid expenses are allocated between the buyer and seller. In most transactions, the seller pays for title insurance and any delinquent assessment liens that would show up as debits. If the seller prepaid the property taxes, he or she would expect to get the unused portion back, which would appear as a credit.

ABC - Assumption by the Buyer is a Credit

When a buyer assumes an existing loan, the assumption is shown on the closing statement as a debit to the seller and a credit to the buyer.

The buyer and seller agree on impound accounts, and the escrow holder is guided on how to handle the credits and debits. An **impound account** is a trust account for funds set aside for future recurring costs relating to a property. After the escrow agent completes the accounting, the agent tells the buyer to deliver the down payment (usually a cashier's check is required), plus other escrow costs, to the escrow office.

At this time, the buyers sign the loan documents and any other paperwork required for the financing is completed. If everything is in order, the loan is funded and the money is sent to the escrow office along with the buyer's funds. Escrow may close at that time.

Audit File

At the close of escrow, the escrow officer must examine each file to assure all accounting is accurate and that escrow instructions have been followed. A cash **reconciliation** statement is completed by the escrow holder and closing statements are prepared for all principals.

Recording

After a final confirmation of the title company records to be sure nothing has changed since the preliminary title search was done, the escrow holder sends all transaction documents (grant deed, trust deed, contract of sale, or option) that need to be recorded to the title company. A title company representative then takes the documents to the county recorder's office and records them. Once the documents are recorded, the escrow officer closes the escrow.

Closing the Escrow

Once all terms and conditions of the escrow instructions have been fulfilled for both parties, the escrow is termed "complete". The last responsibility of the escrow holder is to close the escrow. The escrow officer gives closing statements to the buyer and seller, disburses all money, and delivers all documents to the proper parties after making sure all documents have been recorded by the title company. The seller gets a check for the proceeds of the sale minus escrow fees, real estate commissions, loan payoffs and all other costs of selling, and any pertinent documents; and the buyer gets a grant deed.

Summary

Closing the real estate transaction is the final step on the path that began with a listing agreement. **Closing** is a term that describes the completion of a property transaction. In order to achieve a successful closing, the seller and buyer need to supply certain information, documents, forms, and contracts.

The closing also involves the transfer of funds to finance the real estate transaction. Real estate finance contracts usually involve the borrower of a loan promising to pay back what they owe the lender. The **promissory note** is the evidence of the debt. **Security instruments** are used to secure promissory notes. In Texas, a **deed of trust** is the principal instrument used to secure loans on real property.

Escrow is a closing method that uses a neutral third party (an escrow officer) to coordinate the closing. An escrow is a small and short-lived trust arrangement. The **escrow holder** coordinates communications between the principals, the agents involved, and other professionals (lender, title company, pest control company). Every escrow has two requirements to be valid: a binding contract between the buyer and seller and conditional delivery of transfer documents to a third party.

In Texas, title companies generally handle closings through escrow. In a typical escrow closing, the selling agent opens escrow, the escrow agent prepares escrow instructions, a title search is ordered, and any existing loans are paid off. Reports are then given regarding the condition of the property, the escrow agent accepts loan documents, fire insurance is provided, and a settlement statement is prepared. Finally, the escrow agent audits the file, records title to the property, and the escrow closes.